Work 2.0:

Preparing for the Future Jobs

Preface

Welcome to "Work 2.0: Preparing for the Future Jobs."

The world of work is undergoing a monumental transformation. Technological advancements, the rise of remote work, the gig economy, and unprecedented global events have all contributed to reshaping the landscape of employment. Jobs that were once the cornerstone of our economy are evolving, and new roles are emerging at an unprecedented pace. The future of work is not a distant concept—it is happening now, and it is essential for each of us to be prepared.

This book is designed to be your guide through this transformation. Whether you are a high school student pondering your career choices, a college student about to enter the job market, or a young professional seeking to stay ahead in your field, this book aims to provide you with the knowledge and tools to thrive in the dynamic job market of the future.

We will explore various facets of the evolving work environment, including the remote work revolution, the skills you need to develop for future jobs, the growing gig economy, and the implications of automation and artificial intelligence. We will also delve into the concept of digital nomadism, how organizations are adapting to new work realities, and the crucial collaboration between humans and machines. Furthermore, we will discuss the importance of finding purpose in your work and the lasting changes brought about by the COVID-19 pandemic.

Throughout this journey, you will find practical advice, real-world examples, and motivational insights to help you navigate the future of work. The goal is not only to inform but also to inspire you to take proactive steps in your career development. The future belongs to those who are prepared, adaptable, and resilient.

I invite you to embark on this journey with an open mind and a willingness to embrace change. The future of work is filled with possibilities, and together, we can prepare for the jobs that don't yet exist but will shape our world in the years to come.

Let's dive in and prepare for the exciting future of work.

Bushra Siddiqui

Table of Contents

Chapter 1: The Remote Work Revolution

Chapter 2: Future Skills: Preparing for Jobs That Don't Exist Yet

Chapter 3: The Gig Economy: Flexibility and Freedom

Chapter 4: Automation and AI: Embracing the Future

Chapter 5: Digital Nomadism: Working from Anywhere

Chapter 6: Organizational Adaptation: Building Resilient Workplaces

Chapter 7: Human-Machine Collaboration: The Future of Teamwork

Chapter 8: Purpose-Driven Work: Finding Meaning in Your Career

Chapter 9: Post-Pandemic Changes: Redefining Normal

Chapter 10: Conclusion: Preparing for the Future

Chapter 11: Preparing for an Unpredictable World: Strategies for resilience and Adaptability

Final Reflections

Epilogue

About the Author (s)

Bushra Siddiqui is a dedicated author and sociologist who blends philosophy and social issues into engaging literature. Her latest book, "Work 2.0: Preparing for the Future Jobs," reflects her commitment to providing valuable insights and practical advice for navigating the evolving job market.

Felix McKenzie is a full-time Software Engineer, seasoned writer, and Science Fiction author with over 20 years of experience in the Tech Industry. He is also a career advisor and a science enthusiast, with hobbies including exploring the world and reading and writing on Human Evolution, The Cosmos, and other Science and Technology topics.

Together, Bushra and Felix combine their expertise and passions to offer readers a comprehensive and forward-thinking perspective on the future of work.

Chapter 1: The Remote Work Revolution

Remote Work

Hey there, future remote worker! Did you know that remote work isn't just a trend? It's here to stay. The COVID-19 pandemic fast-tracked the shift to working from home, and many companies have realized that it's not only possible but often beneficial. In fact, remote work has become a significant part of the modern workforce, transforming how businesses operate and how employees manage their professional and personal lives.

But working from home isn't just about wearing pajamas all day. It's about discipline, time management, and creating a productive environment. Let's explore how you can excel in this new way of working, ensuring you're both effective and fulfilled.

The Evolution of Remote Work

To understand the remote work revolution, it's essential to look at its evolution. Remote work isn't a new concept. It dates back to the 1970s when technology began to enable people to work from locations outside the traditional office. However, it wasn't until the advent of the internet, email, and mobile devices that remote work started gaining traction.

The real game-changer was the global COVID-19 pandemic in 2020, which forced millions of people to work from home almost overnight. This sudden shift demonstrated that many jobs could be performed remotely, challenging long-held assumptions about the necessity of physical offices.

Companies like Twitter, Facebook, and Shopify announced permanent shifts to remote or hybrid work models. These decisions reflect a broader trend, as businesses recognize the benefits of remote work, including cost savings on office space, access to a broader talent pool, and improved employee satisfaction.

Setting Up Your Remote Workspace

One of the first steps to successful remote work is setting up a dedicated workspace. Your environment significantly impacts your productivity and well-being. Here are some tips for creating an effective home office:

Choose the Right Spot:

Select a quiet area with minimal distractions. Ideally, this should be a separate room where you can close the door, but if that's not possible, find a corner that you can dedicate to work.

Ergonomic Setup:

Invest in a good chair and desk. Your chair should support your back, and your desk should be at a comfortable height. If possible, use an external monitor, keyboard, and mouse to maintain a healthy posture.

Lighting:

Ensure your workspace has good lighting. Natural light is best, but if that's not an option, use a desk lamp to brighten your area.

Declutter:

Keep your workspace tidy. A clutter-free environment helps reduce stress and increase focus.

Personal Touches:

Add personal items like photos, plants, or artwork to make your space inviting and comfortable.

Establishing a Routine

When you work from home, it's easy for the lines between work and personal life to blur. Establishing a routine can help you maintain a healthy work-life balance. Here's how to create a routine that works for you:

Set Regular Hours:

Define your working hours and stick to them. Whether you're a morning person or a night owl, find the time when you're most productive and build your schedule around it.

Morning Ritual:

Start your day with a morning ritual that signals the beginning of work. This could be as simple as having a cup of coffee, a quick exercise session, or reviewing your to-do list.

Breaks and Lunch:

Schedule regular breaks and a lunch break. Short breaks help you recharge and maintain focus throughout the day. Use tools like the Pomodoro Technique, which involves working for 25 minutes and then taking a 5-minute break.

End-of-Day Routine:

Develop an end-of-day routine to signal the end of your workday. This might include reviewing what you've accomplished, setting priorities for the next day, and shutting down your computer.

Communication and Collaboration

Effective communication is crucial for remote work success. Without face-to-face interactions, staying connected with your team can be challenging. Here are some strategies to ensure clear and consistent communication:

Regular Check-ins:

Schedule regular check-ins with your team. This could be daily stand-up meetings, weekly updates, or bi-weekly one-on-ones. Use video conferencing tools like Zoom, Microsoft Teams, or Google Meet.

Overcommunicate:

In a remote environment, it's better to overcommunicate. Clearly articulate your expectations, deadlines, and any issues you're facing. Use various channels like email, instant messaging, and project management tools.

Collaborative Tools:

Utilize collaborative tools to stay connected. Tools like Slack for instant messaging, Trello or Asana for project management, and Google Drive or Dropbox for file sharing can enhance teamwork and productivity.

Social Interaction:

Don't forget the social aspect of work. Schedule virtual coffee breaks, team-building activities, or informal chat sessions to maintain a sense of camaraderie and connection.

Managing Productivity

Staying productive while working remotely requires discipline and effective time management. Here are some tips to help you stay on track:

Set Clear Goals:

At the beginning of each day or week, set clear, achievable goals. Break larger projects into smaller tasks and prioritize them.

Time Blocking:

Use time blocking to allocate specific periods for different tasks. This helps you focus on one task at a time and avoid multitasking, which can reduce efficiency.

Minimize Distractions:

Identify potential distractions and take steps to minimize them. This could involve setting boundaries with family members, using noise-canceling headphones, or installing productivity apps that block distracting websites.

Use Technology:

Leverage productivity tools and apps. Tools like Todoist for task management, Focus@Will for concentration-enhancing music, and RescueTime for tracking your time can boost your efficiency.

Balancing Work and Personal Life

One of the significant benefits of remote work is the potential for a better work-life balance. However, achieving this balance requires conscious effort. Here are some strategies to help you maintain harmony between your work and personal life:

Set Boundaries:

Clearly define your work hours and communicate them to your family and friends. Let them know when you're not available and when you can be interrupted.

Take Breaks:

Don't neglect breaks. Step away from your desk, go for a walk, stretch, or meditate. Regular breaks help you recharge and prevent burnout.

Exercise and Wellness:

Incorporate exercise into your daily routine. Physical activity boosts your energy, mood, and overall well-being. Consider activities like yoga, jogging, or a home workout.

Unplug After Work:

When your workday ends, unplug from work-related activities. Avoid checking emails or responding to work messages. Spend time on hobbies, with family, or doing things you enjoy.

Overcoming Challenges

Remote work comes with its own set of challenges. Here are some common issues and how to overcome them:

Isolation:

Feeling isolated is a common challenge for remote workers. Combat this by staying connected with your colleagues through virtual meetings and social interactions. Join online communities and networks related to your field.

Communication Barriers:

Miscommunication can occur without face-to-face interactions. Be clear and concise in your communication. Use video calls to convey tone and non-verbal cues.

Tech Issues:

Technical problems can disrupt your workflow. Ensure you have reliable internet, backup your files regularly, and have access to tech support if needed.

Staying Motivated:

Staying motivated can be challenging when working alone. Set personal and professional goals, reward yourself for achieving milestones, and seek feedback and encouragement from your peers.

Case Studies: Success Stories

Let's look at some real-life examples of individuals and companies that have successfully embraced remote work:

GitLab:

GitLab is a fully remote company with over 1,300 employees across 65 countries. They have a robust remote work culture with clear communication guidelines, regular check-ins, and a focus on results rather than hours worked.

Buffer:

Buffer, a social media management platform, has been remote since its inception. They prioritize transparency, team bonding, and continuous learning. Employees are encouraged to take breaks and maintain a healthy work-life balance.

Individual Success: Sarah's Story

Sarah, a marketing professional, transitioned to remote work during the pandemic. She created a dedicated home office, established a routine, and used productivity tools to stay organized. Sarah now enjoys a better work-life balance and has even started a side business.

The Future of Remote Work

The remote work revolution is just beginning. As technology advances and companies continue to embrace flexibility, remote work will become even more prevalent. Here's what the future might hold:

Hybrid Work Models:

Many companies will adopt hybrid work models, allowing employees to work both remotely and in-office. This offers the best of both worlds—flexibility and collaboration.

Global Talent Pool:

Companies can hire talent from anywhere in the world, leading to more diverse and inclusive workplaces. This also means increased competition for jobs, so staying skilled and adaptable is crucial.

Technological Advancements:

Advances in technology, such as virtual reality and AI, will further enhance remote work capabilities. These tools will make remote collaboration even more seamless and effective.

New Job Opportunities:

The rise of remote work will create new job opportunities in fields like remote project management, virtual event planning, and remote team building.

Conclusion

Remote work offers incredible opportunities for flexibility, productivity, and work-life balance. By setting up a dedicated workspace, establishing a routine, and leveraging communication and productivity tools, you can thrive in this new work environment.

Remember, the key to successful remote work is discipline, organization, and continuous learning. Stay connected with your team, set clear goals, and take care of your well-being. Embrace the remote work revolution, and you'll be well-prepared for the future of work.

Chapter 2: Future Skills: Preparing for Jobs That Don't Exist Yet

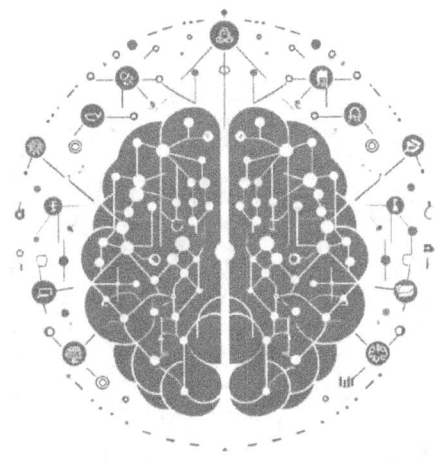

Future Skills

Think about this: many of the jobs that will be in demand in the next 10-20 years don't even exist yet. It sounds daunting, but it's also incredibly exciting. This chapter is dedicated to helping you understand and develop the skills that will keep you relevant in a rapidly changing job market. Whether you're just starting your career or looking to pivot, the key to success lies in continuous learning and adaptability.

The Importance of Lifelong Learning

In the past, education was often seen as a one-time event. You'd go to school, maybe get a degree, and then enter the workforce. Today, this model is obsolete. The pace of technological change means that the skills you learn today might be outdated in a few years. This is why lifelong learning is critical.

Continuous Education:

Embrace a mindset of continuous education. This doesn't necessarily mean formal schooling; it can be online courses, workshops, seminars, and self-study. Platforms like Coursera, Udemy, and Khan Academy offer a wide range of courses on everything from data science to personal development.

Consider obtaining certifications in your field. Certifications can demonstrate your commitment to learning and help you stay current with industry standards.

Staying Curious:

Cultivate curiosity. Ask questions, seek new experiences, and never stop exploring. Curiosity drives innovation and keeps your mind active.

Read widely. Don't just stick to your field; explore other disciplines. This can provide fresh perspectives and innovative solutions to problems.

Digital Literacy: The Foundation of Future Skills

Digital literacy is the ability to use and understand technology effectively. It's the foundation upon which many other future skills are built. In today's world, being digitally literate is as essential as being able to read and write.

Basic Digital Skills:

Start with the basics: proficiency in using computers, smartphones, and other digital devices. Understand how to navigate operating systems, manage files, and use basic software applications.

Learn to troubleshoot common technical issues. Being able to solve minor tech problems can save you time and frustration.

Advanced Digital Skills:

Coding: Learning to code is like learning a new language. It's a valuable skill that can open many doors. Start with languages like Python or JavaScript, which are widely used and beginner-friendly. Websites like Codecademy and FreeCodeCamp offer interactive coding lessons.

Data Analysis: Data is the new oil. Being able to collect, analyze, and interpret data is crucial. Learn to use tools like Excel, SQL, and data visualization software like Tableau.

Digital Marketing: In an increasingly online world, understanding digital marketing is vital. This includes SEO, social media marketing, content creation, and online advertising. Courses on platforms like HubSpot and Google can provide a solid foundation.

Emotional Intelligence: The Human Touch

While technical skills are essential, emotional intelligence (EQ) is equally important. EQ is the ability to understand and manage your own emotions, as well as the emotions of others. In a world where automation and AI are on the rise, emotional intelligence sets you apart.

Self-Awareness:

Reflect on your emotions and how they affect your behavior. Practice mindfulness and meditation to increase self-awareness.

Keep a journal to track your emotional responses and identify patterns.

Self-Regulation:

Learn to manage stress and control impulsive reactions. Techniques like deep breathing, exercise, and time management can help.

Develop resilience by viewing challenges as opportunities for growth.

Empathy:

Put yourself in others' shoes. Practice active listening and show genuine interest in others' feelings and perspectives.

Volunteer or engage in community service to build empathy and understanding.

Social Skills:

Build strong relationships through effective communication and collaboration. Practice giving and receiving feedback constructively.

Work on conflict resolution skills. Approach conflicts with a problem-solving mindset rather than a confrontational one.

Critical Thinking and Problem-Solving

Employers are looking for individuals who can think critically and solve problems creatively. These skills are crucial in navigating the complexities of the modern workplace.

Analyzing Information:

Learn to evaluate information critically. Look for biases, assess the credibility of sources, and consider alternative viewpoints.

Practice breaking down complex problems into smaller, manageable parts.

Creativity and Innovation:

Foster creativity by exploring new ideas and thinking outside the box. Engage in activities like brainstorming, mind mapping, and design thinking.

Embrace failure as a learning opportunity. Don't be afraid to take risks and experiment with new approaches.

Decision-Making:

Develop strong decision-making skills by weighing pros and cons, considering potential outcomes, and consulting with others.

Use tools like SWOT analysis (Strengths, Weaknesses, Opportunities, Threats) to make informed decisions.

Adaptability and Flexibility

The future job market demands adaptability and flexibility. The ability to pivot and learn new skills quickly is invaluable.

Embracing Change:

View change as an opportunity rather than a threat. Stay open-minded and be willing to adjust your plans and goals.

Develop a growth mindset. Believe that your abilities can be developed through dedication and hard work.

Learning New Skills:

Regularly assess your skill set and identify areas for improvement. Set learning goals and create a plan to achieve them.

Take advantage of online resources, workshops, and professional development opportunities to stay current.

Collaboration and Teamwork

The ability to work well with others is crucial, especially in remote and global teams. Effective collaboration enhances productivity and fosters innovation.

Communication:

Practice clear and concise communication. Be mindful of your tone and body language, especially in virtual interactions.

Use collaborative tools like Slack, Microsoft Teams, and Google Drive to facilitate teamwork and information sharing.

Team Building:

Build strong relationships with your colleagues. Participate in team-building activities and social events.

Understand team dynamics and leverage each member's strengths to achieve common goals.

Conflict Resolution:

Approach conflicts with a problem-solving attitude. Focus on finding solutions rather than placing blame.

Develop negotiation skills and learn to compromise when necessary.

Entrepreneurship and Intrapreneurship

In the future job market, entrepreneurial skills will be highly valued, whether you're starting your own business or innovating within an existing company.

Entrepreneurial Mindset:

Develop an entrepreneurial mindset by being proactive, taking initiative, and seeking opportunities for innovation.

Learn about business planning, marketing, and financial management. Resources like the Small Business Administration (SBA) and SCORE offer valuable guidance.

Intrapreneurship:

Embrace intrapreneurship by driving innovation within your organization. Propose new ideas, lead projects, and take ownership of your work.

Foster a culture of creativity and experimentation within your team or department.

Cultural Competence and Global Awareness

As the world becomes more interconnected, cultural competence and global awareness are essential skills. Understanding and respecting different cultures enhances collaboration and opens up new opportunities.

Cultural Awareness:

Educate yourself about different cultures and customs. Travel, if possible, or engage with diverse communities in your area.

Learn to appreciate and respect cultural differences. Avoid making assumptions and ask questions to gain a deeper understanding.

Global Trends:

Stay informed about global trends and events. Read international news, follow global markets, and understand geopolitical issues.

Develop language skills. Learning a new language can enhance your career prospects and enable you to connect with people from different backgrounds.

Case Studies: Real-Life Examples of Future Skills in Action

Let's look at some real-life examples of individuals and companies that have successfully embraced future skills:

Jane's Journey in Digital Literacy:

Jane, a marketing professional, realized the importance of digital literacy early in her career. She took online courses in digital marketing and data analysis, which allowed her to transition into a more tech-focused role within her company. Her ability to interpret data and leverage digital tools made her an invaluable asset to her team.

Mark's Emotional Intelligence Story:

Mark, a project manager, noticed that his team was struggling with communication and conflict. He decided to focus on developing his emotional intelligence. Through mindfulness practices and active listening, he improved his relationships with team members. This change led to a more cohesive and productive team environment.

Sara's Entrepreneurial Success:

Sara, a software developer, had a passion for solving problems creatively. She used her entrepreneurial skills to start her own tech startup, developing innovative solutions for remote work challenges. Her ability to identify opportunities and drive innovation has made her company a leader in its field.

Conclusion: Building Your Future Skillset

As we've explored in this chapter, the future job market requires a diverse set of skills. Digital literacy, emotional intelligence, critical thinking, adaptability, collaboration, entrepreneurship, and cultural competence are all essential for success. By committing to lifelong learning and staying curious, you can prepare yourself for the jobs that don't exist yet.

Remember, the journey to developing these skills is ongoing. Stay proactive, embrace change, and continually seek opportunities to grow. The future of work is full of possibilities, and with the right skills, you can navigate this evolving landscape and achieve your dreams.

By focusing on these future skills, you're not just preparing for a job; you're preparing for a fulfilling and dynamic career. So go out there, embrace the future, and make your mark on the world. The possibilities are endless!

Chapter 3: The Gig Economy: Flexibility and Freedom

The Gig Economy

Welcome to the gig economy, where flexibility and freedom reign supreme! More and more people are choosing freelance and contract work over traditional 9-to-5 jobs. Platforms like Upwork, Fiverr, and TaskRabbit have made it easier than ever to find gigs that match your skills and interests. But what exactly is the gig economy, and why is it becoming such a popular choice for workers and employers alike?

The gig economy is characterized by short-term contracts, freelance work, and independent contracting. It offers unparalleled flexibility, allowing individuals to choose their projects, set their own schedules, and work from anywhere. However, it also comes with its own set of challenges, such as job security, benefits, and consistent income. In this chapter, we'll dive deep into the gig economy, exploring its benefits and challenges, and provide practical advice on how to succeed as a gig worker.

The Rise of the Gig Economy

The gig economy has been growing steadily over the past decade, driven by several factors. Advances in technology, changing attitudes towards work, and economic shifts have all contributed to its rise.

Technological Advances:

The internet, smartphones, and digital platforms have made it easier for people to find and complete freelance work. Websites like Upwork, Fiverr, and TaskRabbit connect freelancers with clients, allowing them to offer their services to a global market.

Communication tools like Zoom, Slack, and email facilitate remote collaboration, making it possible to work with clients and teams from anywhere in the world.

Changing Attitudes Towards Work:

Many people, especially younger generations, are prioritizing work-life balance, flexibility, and autonomy over traditional employment benefits like job security and steady income. The gig economy offers the freedom to choose when, where, and how you work.

There's a growing desire for meaningful work. Freelancing allows individuals to pursue projects they're passionate about, rather than being tied to a single employer.

Economic Shifts:

The global financial crisis and subsequent economic uncertainty have led many people to seek alternative sources of income. Freelancing provides a way to diversify income streams and reduce reliance on a single employer.

Companies are also embracing the gig economy to reduce costs and increase flexibility. Hiring freelancers allows businesses to scale their workforce up or down based on demand without the long-term commitment of traditional employment.

Benefits of the Gig Economy

The gig economy offers numerous benefits for both workers and employers. Here are some of the key advantages:

For Workers:

Flexibility:

One of the most significant benefits of the gig economy is the flexibility it offers. Gig workers can choose their projects, set their own schedules, and work from anywhere. This flexibility allows for a better work-life balance and the ability to pursue other interests or responsibilities.

Autonomy:

Gig workers have control over their careers. They can decide which projects to take on, how much to charge, and how to deliver their services. This autonomy can lead to greater job satisfaction and personal fulfillment.

Diverse Opportunities:

The gig economy offers a wide range of opportunities across various industries. Whether you're a writer, designer, developer, or handyman, there's a gig for you. This diversity allows workers to explore different fields and develop a broad skill set.

Potential for Higher Earnings:

Freelancers often have the potential to earn more than traditional employees, especially if they have specialized skills in high demand. By working with multiple clients and setting their rates, gig workers can maximize their income.

For Employers:

Cost Savings:

Hiring freelancers can be more cost-effective than employing full-time staff. Employers save on benefits, office space, and other overhead costs. Additionally, they can hire freelancers on a project-by-project basis, ensuring they only pay for the work they need.

Access to a Global Talent Pool:

The gig economy allows employers to tap into a global talent pool. They can find specialists and experts from around the world, bringing diverse perspectives and skills to their projects.

Increased Flexibility:

Freelancers provide businesses with the flexibility to scale their workforce up or down based on demand. This agility is particularly beneficial for startups and small businesses that may not have the resources for a full-time staff.

Faster Turnaround:

Freelancers often work on shorter timelines and can complete projects more quickly than in-house teams. This speed can be a significant advantage for businesses looking to move quickly and stay competitive.

Challenges of the Gig Economy

While the gig economy offers many benefits, it also comes with its own set of challenges. Understanding these challenges is crucial for anyone considering a gig career.

For Workers:

Job Security:

One of the biggest challenges of the gig economy is the lack of job security. Freelancers often have to deal with inconsistent income and the uncertainty of finding the next gig. This unpredictability can be stressful and requires careful financial planning.

Benefits and Protections:

Gig workers typically don't receive benefits like health insurance, retirement plans, or paid time off. This lack of benefits can make it challenging to manage healthcare costs and save for the future. Additionally, freelancers are not protected by labor laws that apply to traditional employees.

Work-Life Balance:

While the gig economy offers flexibility, it can also blur the lines between work and personal life. Freelancers may find themselves working long hours to meet deadlines or taking on multiple projects to ensure a steady income. This can lead to burnout if not managed properly.

Self-Management:

Freelancers are responsible for managing every aspect of their business, from marketing and client acquisition to invoicing and taxes. This self-management can be overwhelming, especially for those new to freelancing.

For Employers:

Quality Control:

Ensuring consistent quality can be challenging when working with freelancers. Employers need to invest time in vetting and managing freelancers to ensure they meet the required standards.

Communication:

Effective communication is crucial in the gig economy, especially when working with remote freelancers. Miscommunication can lead to misunderstandings, missed deadlines, and subpar work.

Legal and Compliance Issues:

Employers need to be aware of legal and compliance issues when hiring freelancers. This includes understanding tax implications, contract requirements, and intellectual property rights.

Integration with In-House Teams:

Integrating freelancers with in-house teams can be challenging. Employers need to ensure that freelancers have access to the necessary resources and are aligned with the company's goals and culture.

Succeeding in the Gig Economy

To succeed in the gig economy, it's essential to be proactive, disciplined, and strategic. Here are some practical tips to help you thrive as a gig worker:

Building a Strong Personal Brand:

Create a Professional Online Presence:

Your online presence is often the first impression potential clients will have of you. Create a professional LinkedIn profile that highlights your skills, experience, and achievements. A personal website or portfolio showcasing your work can also help you stand out.

Networking:

Networking is crucial in the gig economy. Connect with potential clients, industry peers, and other freelancers. Attend industry events, join online communities, and participate in social media groups related to your field.

Showcase Your Expertise:

Establish yourself as an expert in your field by sharing your knowledge and insights. Write blog posts, create video content, or offer webinars. This can help you build credibility and attract clients.

Time Management and Organization:

Set Clear Goals:

Define your short-term and long-term goals. Having clear objectives will help you stay focused and motivated. Break larger goals into smaller, manageable tasks.

Use Productivity Tools:

Utilize productivity tools like Trello, Asana, and Google Calendar to manage your projects and deadlines. Time tracking apps like Toggl can help you monitor how you're spending your time and identify areas for improvement.

Create a Routine:

Establish a daily routine that works for you. Consistency can help you stay productive and maintain a work-life balance. Schedule regular breaks to recharge and avoid burnout.

Financial Management:

Budgeting:

Create a budget that accounts for your income and expenses. Track your earnings and expenditures to ensure you're living within your means. Set aside money for taxes, healthcare, and emergencies.

Saving and Investing:

Save a portion of your income for future goals and unexpected expenses. Consider opening a retirement account and investing in a diversified portfolio to build long-term wealth.

Invoicing and Payments:

Use invoicing software to streamline your billing process. Clearly outline payment terms in your contracts and follow up on overdue invoices promptly. Consider using escrow services for larger projects to ensure timely payments.

Continuous Learning and Skill Development:

Stay Updated:

The gig economy is dynamic, and staying updated with industry trends and developments is crucial. Follow industry news, subscribe to relevant newsletters, and participate in online courses.

Expand Your Skill Set:

Continuously improve your existing skills and learn new ones. Platforms like Coursera, Udemy, and LinkedIn Learning offer a wide range of courses. Consider obtaining certifications in areas that are in high demand.

Seek Feedback:

Actively seek feedback from clients and peers to improve your work. Constructive criticism can help you identify areas for growth and enhance your services.

Building Client Relationships:

Deliver Quality Work:

Consistently delivering high-quality work is the best way to build a strong reputation and attract repeat clients. Pay attention to detail, meet deadlines, and exceed client expectations.

Communication:

Maintain clear and open communication with your clients. Keep them updated on project progress, respond to inquiries promptly, and address any concerns they may have.

Client Retention:

Building long-term relationships with clients can provide a steady stream of work. Offer excellent customer service, show appreciation, and follow up after project completion to stay top-of-mind.

Case Studies: Success Stories in the Gig Economy

Let's look at some real-life examples of individuals and companies that have successfully embraced the gig economy:

Anna the Freelance Graphic Designer:

Anna, a freelance graphic designer, built her career from the ground up. She started by creating a professional online portfolio showcasing her work. Through networking and leveraging platforms like Upwork and Fiverr, she landed her first few clients. Anna focused on delivering high-quality work and building strong client relationships. Over time, she established herself as a reputable designer, attracting high-profile clients and earning a steady income. Her success is a testament to the power of a strong personal brand and continuous learning.

David's Journey in Content Writing:

David, a freelance content writer, transitioned from a traditional job to freelancing after realizing his passion for writing. He began by writing blog posts for small businesses and gradually expanded his services to include SEO content, whitepapers, and e-books. David utilized productivity tools to manage his time effectively and continuously sought feedback to improve his writing. By networking and showcasing his expertise through a personal blog, David built a loyal client base and achieved financial stability.

TechHub: A Success Story in the Gig Economy:

TechHub, a startup focused on providing IT solutions, embraced the gig economy to scale its operations. Instead of hiring full-time staff, TechHub contracted freelancers for various projects, from software development to digital marketing. This approach allowed the company to access a global talent pool and maintain flexibility. By using collaborative tools and establishing clear communication channels, TechHub ensured consistent quality and timely delivery. The company's success highlights the benefits of leveraging the gig economy for business growth.

Conclusion: Embracing the Gig Economy

The gig economy offers incredible opportunities for flexibility, autonomy, and diverse experiences. By building a strong personal brand, managing your time effectively, and continuously improving your skills, you can thrive as a gig worker. Understand the challenges, plan for them, and leverage the benefits to create a fulfilling and successful freelance career.

Remember, the key to succeeding in the gig economy is proactive planning, disciplined execution, and a willingness to adapt. Embrace the freedom and flexibility it offers, and you'll be well-prepared to navigate this dynamic and exciting landscape. The future of work is here, and with the right approach, you can make the gig economy work for you.

Chapter 4: Automation and AI: Embracing the Future

Automation and AI

The robots are coming, but don't worry—they're here to help! Automation and artificial intelligence (AI) are transforming industries, making processes more efficient, and creating new job opportunities. In this chapter, we'll explore how automation and AI are shaping the future, the potential impact on the job market, and how you can prepare for these changes.

Automation and AI are not just buzzwords; they are powerful technologies that are already integrated into many aspects of our daily lives and work environments. From chatbots handling customer service inquiries to AI-driven algorithms predicting market trends, these technologies are redefining how we live and work. Let's dive into the world of AI and automation to understand their potential and prepare for the future.

Understanding Artificial Intelligence

Artificial intelligence is a branch of computer science focused on creating systems capable of performing tasks that typically require human intelligence. These tasks include learning, reasoning, problem-solving, perception, and language understanding. AI can be broadly categorized into two types: narrow AI and general AI.

Narrow AI:

Narrow AI, also known as weak AI, is designed to perform specific tasks. Examples include voice assistants like Siri and Alexa, recommendation algorithms on Netflix and Amazon, and image recognition systems used in medical diagnostics. Narrow AI excels in its designated tasks but cannot perform outside its scope.

General AI:

General AI, also known as strong AI or artificial general intelligence (AGI), refers to systems that possess human-like intelligence and can perform any intellectual task that a human can. AGI remains a theoretical concept, and while it is the ultimate goal of AI research, it is still far from being realized.

How AI Works: The Basics

To understand AI, it's essential to grasp the basics of how it works. AI systems rely on vast amounts of data, advanced algorithms, and powerful computing resources to function. Here's a simplified overview of the key components:

Data:

Data is the fuel for AI systems. The more data an AI system has, the better it can learn and perform. This data can come from various sources, including text, images, videos, and real-time inputs.

Algorithms:

Algorithms are the instructions that tell an AI system how to analyze data and make decisions. Machine learning algorithms, a subset of AI, enable systems to learn from data and improve over time without being explicitly programmed.

Computing Power:

AI requires significant computational power to process large datasets and run complex algorithms. Advances in hardware, such as GPUs (Graphics Processing Units) and TPUs (Tensor Processing

Units), have made it possible to build and deploy sophisticated AI systems.

Training and Testing:

AI systems go through a process of training and testing. During training, the system learns from historical data to recognize patterns and make predictions. Testing involves evaluating the system's performance on new data to ensure accuracy and reliability.

Prompts and Natural Language Processing (NLP)

One of the most exciting developments in AI is the ability to understand and generate human language through natural language processing (NLP). NLP enables machines to read, interpret, and respond to human language in a way that feels natural and intuitive.

Prompts:

Prompts are inputs or queries provided to an AI system to elicit a response. In the context of language models like ChatGPT, prompts can be questions, statements, or commands that the AI uses to generate relevant and coherent responses.

For example, if you ask, "What is the capital of France?" the AI processes the prompt and responds with "Paris."

ChatGPT:

ChatGPT, developed by OpenAI, is an advanced language model that uses deep learning techniques to generate human-like text. It can engage in conversations, answer questions, write essays, and even create poetry.

ChatGPT is based on the GPT (Generative Pre-trained Transformer) architecture, which is trained on diverse datasets to understand and generate text. It can adapt to different contexts and provide relevant responses based on the input it receives.

The Impact of AI on the Job Market

AI and automation are poised to revolutionize the job market, creating new opportunities while rendering some traditional roles obsolete. Understanding this impact is crucial for preparing for the future.

Job Displacement:

Certain jobs, especially those involving repetitive and manual tasks, are at risk of being automated. Examples include assembly line work, data entry, and routine administrative tasks. Automation can perform these tasks more efficiently and accurately, leading to job displacement in these areas.

Job Creation:

While AI and automation may displace some jobs, they will also create new opportunities in fields such as AI development, data science, cybersecurity, and AI ethics. These roles require specialized skills and knowledge, highlighting the importance of continuous learning and upskilling.

Augmented Roles:

Many jobs will be augmented rather than replaced by AI. In these roles, AI will assist humans in performing tasks more effectively. For example, in healthcare, AI can analyze medical images to help doctors diagnose diseases, while in finance, AI can provide insights to assist financial analysts in making informed decisions.

Shift in Skill Demand:

The demand for skills will shift from manual and routine tasks to cognitive and analytical abilities. Skills such as critical thinking, problem-solving, creativity, and emotional intelligence will become increasingly valuable in the AI-driven job market.

Preparing for an AI-Driven Future

The future job market will be shaped by AI and automation. Here are some suggestions to help you prepare for the uncertainty and thrive in an AI-driven world:

Embrace Lifelong Learning:

Continuous learning is essential in an AI-driven world. Stay curious and open to new knowledge. Take online courses, attend workshops, and read extensively to keep your skills up-to-date.

Develop Technical Skills:

Gain a basic understanding of AI and machine learning. Learn to code in languages like Python, which is widely used in AI development. Familiarize yourself with data analysis tools and techniques.

Enhance Soft Skills:

Focus on developing soft skills such as communication, teamwork, and adaptability. These skills will remain valuable as they complement the capabilities of AI and automation.

Stay Informed:

Keep up with the latest developments in AI and automation. Follow industry news, join online communities, and participate in discussions to stay informed about trends and innovations.

Be Adaptable:

Embrace change and be willing to pivot your career as needed. The ability to adapt to new roles and industries will be crucial in navigating the evolving job market.

Hypothetical Future Scenarios

Let's explore some hypothetical future scenarios to understand how AI might shape the job market and daily life:

Scenario 1: AI in Healthcare:

In the future, AI-powered systems could revolutionize healthcare. Imagine an AI assistant that can analyze medical records, predict potential health issues, and recommend personalized treatment plans. Doctors and nurses would collaborate with AI to provide more accurate and efficient care, leading to better patient outcomes.

Scenario 2: AI in Education:

AI could transform education by offering personalized learning experiences. Students could have AI tutors that adapt to their learning styles and pace, providing targeted support and resources. Teachers would focus on mentoring and facilitating collaborative projects, enhancing the overall learning experience.

Scenario 3: AI in Transportation:

Autonomous vehicles could become the norm, reducing traffic accidents and improving transportation efficiency. AI-powered logistics systems would optimize delivery routes, reducing costs and environmental impact. This would create new jobs in AI maintenance, programming, and system design.

Scenario 4: AI in Creative Industries:

AI could assist in creative processes, such as writing, music composition, and visual arts. Imagine an AI collaborator that helps writers generate ideas, musicians create melodies, or artists design digital artwork. This would enable creatives to push the boundaries of their work and explore new possibilities.

Preparing for Uncertainty

While AI offers exciting possibilities, it also brings uncertainty. Here are some strategies to help you navigate this uncertainty:

Build a Diverse Skill Set:

Develop a broad range of skills to increase your adaptability. Combining technical, cognitive, and soft skills will make you more resilient in the face of change.

Stay Agile:

Be open to new opportunities and willing to pivot your career. Embrace a growth mindset and view challenges as opportunities for growth and learning.

Network and Collaborate:

Build a strong professional network. Connect with others in your field, attend industry events, and join online communities. Collaboration and networking can provide support and open doors to new opportunities.

Plan for Financial Security:

Save and invest wisely to build financial security. Diversify your income streams and consider creating passive income sources to reduce reliance on a single job.

Focus on Well-Being:

Prioritize your mental and physical well-being. Practice self-care, maintain a healthy work-life balance, and seek support when needed. A healthy, balanced life will help you navigate uncertainty more effectively.

Conclusion: Embracing AI and Automation

AI and automation are transforming the world, creating new opportunities and challenges. By understanding these technologies and preparing for the future, you can navigate the evolving job market with confidence. Embrace lifelong learning, develop a diverse skill set, and stay adaptable to thrive in an AI-driven world.

Remember, the key to success in an AI-driven future is not just technical skills but also the ability to think critically, communicate effectively, and adapt to change. The future is full of possibilities, and with the right approach, you can make the most of the opportunities that AI and automation bring.

So, embrace the future, stay curious, and prepare for the exciting journey ahead. The world of AI and automation awaits, and you have the power to shape your path and achieve your dreams.

Chapter 5: Digital Nomadism: Working from Anywhere

Digital Nomadism

Imagine working from a beach in Bali, a café in Paris, or a mountain cabin in Colorado. Welcome to the life of a digital nomad! This lifestyle offers the ultimate freedom to work from anywhere in the world, as long as you have a reliable internet connection. In this chapter, we'll explore the rise of digital nomadism, its benefits and challenges, and provide practical advice on how to succeed as a digital nomad.

Digital nomadism combines remote work with travel, allowing individuals to explore new places while maintaining their careers. This lifestyle is becoming increasingly popular, driven by advances in technology, the rise of remote work, and a desire for adventure and flexibility. Let's dive into the world of digital nomadism and discover how you can embrace this exciting way of life.

The Rise of Digital Nomadism

Digital nomadism has been around for decades, but it has gained significant traction in recent years. Several factors have contributed to its rise:

Technological Advances:

The internet, laptops, and smartphones have made it possible to work from almost anywhere. Cloud-based tools and communication platforms like Slack, Zoom, and Google Drive facilitate remote collaboration and project management.

High-speed internet is increasingly available in more locations worldwide, making it easier for digital nomads to stay connected and productive.

Remote Work Revolution:

The COVID-19 pandemic accelerated the shift to remote work, proving that many jobs can be done outside of traditional office settings. Companies have realized the benefits of remote work, such as increased productivity and reduced overhead costs, leading to more remote job opportunities.

Changing Attitudes Towards Work:

Many people, especially millennials and Gen Z, prioritize experiences and flexibility over traditional career paths. Digital nomadism offers the freedom to travel, explore new cultures, and live life on their terms while maintaining a career.

Globalization:

The world is becoming more interconnected, with easier access to travel and a growing number of international communities. This globalization has made it more feasible for individuals to live and work in different countries.

Benefits of Digital Nomadism

Digital nomadism offers numerous benefits, making it an attractive lifestyle choice for many:

For Digital Nomads:

Flexibility and Freedom:

Digital nomads have the freedom to choose where they live and work. This flexibility allows for a better work-life balance and the opportunity to explore new places and cultures.

Personal Growth:

Living and working in different environments can lead to personal growth and development. Digital nomads often become more adaptable, resourceful, and open-minded.

Cost Savings:

In some cases, digital nomads can save money by living in countries with a lower cost of living. This can allow them to stretch their income further and enjoy a higher quality of life.

Enhanced Creativity:

Experiencing new cultures and environments can inspire creativity and innovation. Digital nomads often find that their work benefits from the diverse perspectives and experiences they encounter.

For Employers:

Access to a Global Talent Pool:

Employers can hire talent from anywhere in the world, bringing diverse skills and perspectives to their teams. This can lead to more innovative solutions and a competitive edge.

Increased Productivity:

Studies have shown that remote workers are often more productive than their office-based counterparts. Digital nomads, in particular, tend to be highly motivated and efficient.

Cost Savings:

Employers can save on office space, utilities, and other overhead costs by hiring remote workers. This can lead to significant savings, especially for startups and small businesses.

Employee Satisfaction:

Offering remote work and digital nomad opportunities can increase employee satisfaction and retention. Workers who have the flexibility to live and work where they choose are often more engaged and loyal.

Challenges of Digital Nomadism

While digital nomadism offers many benefits, it also comes with its own set of challenges. Understanding these challenges is crucial for anyone considering this lifestyle:

For Digital Nomads:

Work-Life Balance:

Maintaining a healthy work-life balance can be challenging when you're constantly on the move. Digital nomads need to establish routines and boundaries to ensure they're productive while still enjoying their travels.

Loneliness and Isolation:

Traveling and working alone can be isolating. Digital nomads often miss out on the social interactions and support systems that come with traditional work environments. Building a network of fellow nomads and joining coworking spaces can help mitigate this.

Legal and Financial Issues:

Navigating visas, taxes, and legal requirements can be complex for digital nomads. It's essential to research and understand the regulations of the countries you plan to visit and work in.

Health and Well-being:

Staying healthy while traveling can be challenging. Digital nomads need to prioritize their physical and mental well-being, ensuring they have access to healthcare and maintain a balanced lifestyle.

For Employers:

Communication and Collaboration:

Ensuring effective communication and collaboration can be challenging with remote teams spread across different time zones. Employers need to invest in tools and strategies to facilitate seamless interactions.

Trust and Accountability:

Building trust and ensuring accountability can be more difficult with remote workers. Employers need to establish clear expectations, regular check-ins, and performance metrics to manage remote teams effectively.

Cultural Differences:

Working with a global team can lead to cultural misunderstandings and differences in work styles. Employers need to foster an inclusive culture and provide training to bridge these gaps.

Legal and Compliance Issues:

Employers must navigate the legal and compliance issues associated with hiring remote workers in different countries. This includes understanding tax implications, labor laws, and data protection regulations.

Succeeding as a Digital Nomad

To succeed as a digital nomad, it's essential to be proactive, organized, and adaptable. Here are some practical tips to help you thrive in this lifestyle:

Securing Remote Work:

Find Remote Job Opportunities:

Look for remote job opportunities on websites like Remote.co, We Work Remotely, and FlexJobs. These platforms specialize in connecting remote workers with employers.

Consider freelancing or starting your own business. Platforms like Upwork, Fiverr, and Freelancer can help you find freelance gigs, while starting your own business allows for even greater flexibility.

Negotiate Remote Work with Your Employer:

If you're currently employed, consider negotiating a remote work arrangement with your employer. Present a well-thought-out plan highlighting the benefits of remote work and how you'll maintain productivity and communication.

Planning Your Travels:

Choose Your Destinations Wisely:

Research destinations with reliable internet, a low cost of living, and a supportive digital nomad community. Websites like Nomad List can help you find the best spots.

Consider factors like climate, time zone, and safety when choosing your destinations. It's essential to find a place that aligns with your work schedule and lifestyle preferences.

Stay Organized:

Create a travel itinerary and keep track of important documents, such as visas, passports, and travel insurance. Use apps like TripIt and Google Keep to stay organized.

Plan your accommodation in advance. Websites like Airbnb, Booking.com, and local coworking spaces often offer long-term rental options for digital nomads.

Staying Productive:

Establish a Routine:

Create a daily routine that works for you. Consistency can help you stay productive and maintain a work-life balance. Schedule regular breaks to recharge and avoid burnout.

Set specific work hours and stick to them. This will help you establish boundaries and ensure you're productive during your work time.

Find a Suitable Workspace:

Choose a workspace that's conducive to productivity. This could be a coworking space, a café with good Wi-Fi, or a quiet corner of your accommodation.

Invest in noise-canceling headphones and portable office equipment, such as a laptop stand and an external keyboard, to create a comfortable and efficient workspace.

Maintaining Work-Life Balance:

Set Boundaries:

Clearly define your work hours and communicate them to your clients, colleagues, and travel companions. Let them know when you're available and when you need to focus on work.

Take regular breaks to rest and recharge. Use techniques like the Pomodoro Technique, which involves working for 25 minutes and then taking a 5-minute break.

Prioritize Self-Care:

Take care of your physical and mental well-being. Stay active by incorporating exercise into your daily routine, whether it's going for a run, practicing yoga, or exploring your surroundings.

Practice mindfulness and relaxation techniques, such as meditation and deep breathing exercises, to reduce stress and maintain mental clarity.

Building a Support Network:

Connect with Other Digital Nomads:

Join online communities and social media groups for digital nomads. These platforms can provide support, advice, and networking opportunities.

Attend digital nomad meetups and events in your destination. Coworking spaces often host networking events and social gatherings for remote workers.

Stay Connected with Friends and Family:

Maintain regular communication with your friends and family back home. Use video calls, messaging apps, and social media to stay in touch and share your experiences.

Building a support network can help you combat loneliness and stay motivated on your journey.

Navigating Legal and Financial Issues:

Research Visa Requirements:

Understand the visa requirements for the countries you plan to visit. Some countries offer digital nomad visas, which allow remote workers to live and work legally for an extended period.

Plan your travel itinerary to ensure you comply with visa regulations and avoid overstaying.

Manage Your Finances:

Keep track of your income and expenses using budgeting apps like Mint or YNAB. Save and invest wisely to build financial security.

Understand the tax implications of working remotely. Consult a tax professional to ensure you're compliant with tax regulations in your home country and the countries you visit.

Staying Healthy:

Access to Healthcare:

Research healthcare options in your destination. Ensure you have access to medical facilities and emergency services if needed.

Consider purchasing travel health insurance to cover medical expenses and emergencies while you're abroad.

Healthy Lifestyle:

Maintain a balanced diet and stay hydrated. Explore local markets and try fresh, nutritious foods.

Prioritize sleep and rest. Ensure you get enough sleep to stay energized and focused.

Case Studies: Success Stories in Digital Nomadism

Let's look at some real-life examples of individuals who have successfully embraced the digital nomad lifestyle:

Emily the Remote Marketer:

Emily, a digital marketing specialist, decided to leave her corporate job and embrace digital nomadism. She negotiated a remote work arrangement with her employer and started traveling to different countries. Emily established a routine, joined coworking spaces, and connected with other digital nomads. Her productivity increased, and she enjoyed the freedom to explore new cultures. Emily's success highlights the benefits of flexibility and networking.

James the Freelance Developer:

James, a freelance web developer, built his career by taking on projects through platforms like Upwork and Freelancer. He planned his travels to destinations with reliable internet and a low cost of living. James created a comfortable workspace and maintained a consistent work schedule. By joining digital nomad communities and attending meetups, he built a strong support network. James's story demonstrates the importance of planning and staying connected.

Preeti's Entrepreneurial Journey:

Preeti, an entrepreneur, started her own online business while traveling the world. She leveraged social media and digital marketing to grow her business and attract clients. Preeti balanced work and travel by setting boundaries and prioritizing self-care. She explored new destinations, experienced different cultures, and built a successful business. Preeti's journey showcases the potential for personal and professional growth as a digital nomad.

Conclusion: Embracing Digital Nomadism

Digital nomadism offers incredible opportunities for flexibility, personal growth, and adventure. By securing remote work, planning your travels, and staying productive, you can thrive as a digital nomad. Understand the challenges, plan for them, and leverage the benefits to create a fulfilling and successful lifestyle.

Remember, the key to succeeding as a digital nomad is proactive planning, disciplined execution, and a willingness to adapt. Embrace the freedom and flexibility it offers, and you'll be well-prepared to navigate this dynamic and exciting lifestyle. The future of work is here, and with the right approach, you can make digital nomadism work for you.

So, pack your bags, grab your laptop, and get ready to embark on an incredible journey. The world is your office, and the possibilities are endless. Embrace the digital nomad lifestyle, and you'll discover a world of opportunities and experiences waiting for you.

Chapter 6: Organizational Adaptation: Building Resilient Workplaces

A New Era of Workplaces

Hey there, trailblazer! You've journeyed through the realms of remote work, future skills, gig economy, AI, and digital nomadism. Now, it's time to shift gears and focus on how organizations are transforming to keep pace with these changes. Picture this: a vibrant workplace buzzing with innovation, where creativity flows freely, and adaptability is the norm. Welcome to the new era of resilient workplaces!

Organizations are evolving to meet the demands of a dynamic workforce and an ever-changing market. This chapter will take you on a thrilling ride through the world of organizational adaptation. We'll explore how companies are redefining their structures, embracing flexibility, fostering a culture of continuous learning, and leveraging technology to stay ahead. And to keep things exciting, we'll weave in some fictional stories that bring these concepts to life.

The Flexible Organization

Let's start with flexibility. Imagine a company where employees choose their work hours, collaborate across time zones, and innovate from the comfort of their homes. This isn't a far-fetched dream; it's becoming the new reality. Organizations are moving away from rigid structures and adopting flexible work models that cater to the diverse needs of their workforce.

Case Study: The FlexiCorp Adventure

Meet FlexiCorp, a tech startup founded by visionary entrepreneur Maya. Maya's mission is to create a company where employees have the freedom to work when and where they're most productive. FlexiCorp's team is spread across the globe, from developers in India to marketers in Brazil.

At FlexiCorp, there are no fixed office hours. Employees set their schedules based on their peak productivity times. Maya believes in results over hours worked. The team uses project management tools like Trello to track progress and communicate through Slack and Zoom. This flexible approach has led to higher job satisfaction, increased creativity, and a stronger sense of ownership among employees.

Embracing a Culture of Continuous Learning

In a rapidly changing world, the ability to learn and adapt is crucial. Organizations are fostering a culture of continuous learning to stay competitive. This involves providing employees with opportunities for professional development, encouraging knowledge sharing, and promoting a growth mindset.

Case Study: The Learning Odyssey at Innovate Inc.

Innovate Inc., a global consultancy firm, is renowned for its commitment to employee development. Under the leadership of CEO Alex, the company has created the Innovate Academy, a comprehensive learning platform offering courses in leadership, technology, and soft skills.

Employees at Innovate Inc. are encouraged to spend 20% of their work hours on learning and development. They have access to online courses, workshops, and mentoring programs. The company also hosts monthly knowledge-sharing sessions where employees present their learnings and insights.

Alex's vision is to create a learning organization where employees are empowered to take charge of their growth. This investment in continuous learning has paid off, with Innovate Inc. consistently ranking as one of the top consultancies in the industry.

Technology and Automation: The Digital Transformation

Technology is the backbone of modern organizations. From AI-driven analytics to cloud computing, companies are leveraging technology to streamline operations, enhance decision-making, and drive innovation.

Case Study: The Digital Renaissance at TechSolutions

TechSolutions, a leading IT services company, was facing stiff competition and declining market share. CEO Jordan knew that a digital transformation was essential to regain their edge. The company embarked on a journey to integrate cutting-edge technology into every aspect of their operations.

TechSolutions adopted AI-driven analytics to gain deeper insights into customer behavior. They implemented cloud-based collaboration tools to enhance remote work and used automation to streamline repetitive tasks. The digital transformation not only improved efficiency but also unlocked new revenue streams through innovative products and services.

Jordan's bold vision and the company's commitment to embracing technology turned TechSolutions into a market leader once again. The digital renaissance at TechSolutions serves as a powerful example of how technology can drive organizational success.

Fostering Innovation and Creativity

Innovation is the lifeblood of any successful organization. Companies are creating environments that nurture creativity, encourage experimentation, and embrace failure as a learning opportunity.

Case Study: The Innovation Labs at CreativeCorp

CreativeCorp, a global design agency, is renowned for its groundbreaking work and innovative solutions. The company's secret sauce is the Innovation Labs, a dedicated space where employees are free to experiment, brainstorm, and prototype new ideas.

Under the leadership of Chief Innovation Officer Emma, CreativeCorp encourages employees to spend 10% of their work hours on passion projects. These projects often lead to innovative solutions that the company later develops and markets.

The Innovation Labs are equipped with the latest technology and resources, from 3D printers to virtual reality headsets. Employees are encouraged to collaborate across disciplines, bringing together designers, engineers, and marketers to solve complex problems.

Emma's approach to fostering innovation has made CreativeCorp a trendsetter in the industry, with clients lining up for their cutting-edge designs and creative solutions.

Building a Resilient Culture

Resilience is about more than just bouncing back from setbacks; it's about thriving in the face of challenges. Organizations are focusing on building resilient cultures that empower employees, promote well-being, and create a sense of belonging.

Case Study: The Resilience Revolution at HealthPlus

HealthPlus, a leading healthcare provider, faced unprecedented challenges during the global pandemic. CEO Lisa knew that building a resilient culture was essential to navigate the crisis and emerge stronger.

Lisa launched the Resilience Revolution initiative, focusing on three key pillars: employee well-being, empowerment, and community. HealthPlus provided employees with access to mental health resources, flexible work arrangements, and wellness programs.

To empower employees, Lisa introduced a decentralized decision-making model, allowing frontline workers to make critical decisions quickly. The company also fostered a strong sense of community through virtual town halls, support groups, and volunteer opportunities.

The Resilience Revolution transformed HealthPlus into a more agile and compassionate organization, better equipped to serve its patients and support its employees.

Collaboration and Communication: Breaking Down Silos

Effective collaboration and communication are essential for organizational success. Companies are breaking down silos, fostering cross-functional teams, and using technology to enhance communication.

Case Study: The Collaborative Culture at UnityTech

UnityTech, a multinational technology company, struggled with communication and collaboration across its global offices. CEO Rafael implemented a new strategy to create a more cohesive and collaborative culture.

Rafael introduced cross-functional teams to work on key projects, bringing together employees from different departments and regions. These teams used collaboration tools like Microsoft Teams and Miro to brainstorm, plan, and execute their projects.

UnityTech also adopted a transparent communication policy, with regular updates from leadership and open forums for employees to share their ideas and concerns. Rafael's commitment to fostering collaboration and communication transformed UnityTech into a more unified and innovative organization.

The Power of Diversity and Inclusion

Diversity and inclusion are critical for fostering innovation and driving organizational success. Companies are embracing diverse perspectives and creating inclusive environments where everyone feels valued and respected.

Case Study: The Inclusion Initiative at GlobalReach

GlobalReach, an international logistics company, recognized the need for greater diversity and inclusion within its workforce. Under the leadership of Chief Diversity Officer Nina, the company launched the Inclusion Initiative.

The Inclusion Initiative focused on recruiting diverse talent, providing bias training, and creating employee resource groups.

GlobalReach also implemented policies to ensure equal opportunities for advancement and fostered a culture of respect and belonging.

Nina's efforts led to a more diverse and inclusive workforce, driving innovation and improving employee satisfaction. The Inclusion Initiative made GlobalReach a more competitive and socially responsible company.

Preparing for the Future: Agility and Adaptability

The future is unpredictable, and organizations must be agile and adaptable to thrive. This involves being open to change, continuously monitoring the external environment, and being ready to pivot when necessary.

Case Study: The Agility Advantage at FutureTech

FutureTech, a cutting-edge robotics company, faced rapid changes in technology and market demands. CEO Ethan knew that agility was essential to stay ahead of the competition.

Ethan implemented the Agility Advantage program, focusing on three key areas: rapid decision-making, continuous improvement, and proactive change management. FutureTech adopted agile methodologies, allowing teams to iterate quickly and respond to feedback.

The company also established a culture of continuous improvement, encouraging employees to identify and implement process enhancements. Regular scenario planning and risk assessments ensured that FutureTech was prepared for potential disruptions.

The Agility Advantage program positioned FutureTech as a leader in the robotics industry, ready to adapt to whatever the future might bring.

Conclusion: Embracing Organizational Adaptation

Organizations must embrace change to thrive in the modern world. By adopting flexible work models, fostering a culture of continuous learning, leveraging technology, and building resilient cultures, companies can navigate the complexities of today's market.

Remember, the key to organizational adaptation is creating an environment that empowers employees, encourages innovation, and embraces diversity and inclusion. As a leader or aspiring leader, you have the power to drive this transformation and build a resilient workplace that stands the test of time.

So, get ready to ignite the spark of change within your organization. Embrace the future with confidence, and lead the charge towards a more flexible, innovative, and resilient workplace. The journey ahead is full of possibilities, and with the right approach, you can shape a thriving organization that inspires and empowers everyone within it.

Chapter 7: Human-Machine Collaboration: The Future of Teamwork

The New Age of Collaboration

Welcome, forward-thinker! As we venture deeper into the future of work, we find ourselves at the intersection of human ingenuity and machine intelligence. Imagine a world where humans and machines work together seamlessly, enhancing each other's capabilities and achieving what was once thought impossible. This is not science fiction; it's the emerging reality of human-machine collaboration.

In this chapter, we'll explore how artificial intelligence (AI) and automation are transforming teamwork. We'll delve into the benefits and challenges of this collaboration, provide real-world examples, and offer insights on how to thrive in this new paradigm. Get ready to be inspired and equipped with the knowledge to harness the power of human-machine collaboration.

Understanding Human-Machine Collaboration

Human-machine collaboration refers to the partnership between humans and intelligent machines to accomplish tasks, solve problems, and innovate. This collaboration leverages the strengths of both parties: human creativity, empathy, and critical thinking, combined with machine precision, speed, and data processing power.

The Roles of Humans and Machines:

Humans bring creativity, emotional intelligence, and complex problem-solving abilities to the table. We excel at tasks that require empathy, ethical judgment, and innovative thinking.

Machines, particularly AI, can process vast amounts of data quickly, perform repetitive tasks with high accuracy, and identify patterns that might elude human perception. They are invaluable in areas such as data analysis, automation, and routine decision-making.

Benefits of Human-Machine Collaboration

The synergy between humans and machines offers numerous benefits, enhancing productivity, innovation, and job satisfaction. Here are some key advantages:

Enhanced Productivity:

Machines can handle repetitive and time-consuming tasks, freeing up humans to focus on more strategic and creative activities. This division of labor increases overall productivity and efficiency.

Improved Decision-Making:

AI systems can analyze large datasets and provide insights that inform human decision-making. This data-driven approach leads to more accurate and effective decisions.

Innovation and Creativity:

Human creativity is amplified when supported by AI tools. Machines can generate ideas, identify trends, and offer suggestions that spark human innovation.

Greater Accuracy and Precision:

Machines excel at tasks that require precision and consistency. By handling these tasks, AI reduces the risk of human error and ensures high-quality outcomes.

Scalability:

AI systems can scale operations quickly and handle increased workloads without compromising performance. This scalability is particularly beneficial for businesses experiencing rapid growth.

Challenges of Human-Machine Collaboration

While the benefits are significant, human-machine collaboration also presents challenges that must be addressed to maximize its potential. These challenges include:

Trust and Acceptance:

Building trust in AI systems is crucial for effective collaboration. Humans must understand and trust the capabilities and limitations of AI to work effectively with machines.

Skill Gaps:

There is a need for new skills and competencies to work alongside AI. Employees must be trained in AI tools and technologies, as well as in interpreting and leveraging AI-generated insights.

Ethical Considerations:

The use of AI raises ethical questions around bias, privacy, and accountability. Organizations must establish ethical guidelines and frameworks to ensure responsible AI use.

Integration and Interoperability:

Integrating AI systems with existing processes and technologies can be complex. Ensuring interoperability and seamless integration is essential for smooth collaboration.

Change Management:

Adapting to human-machine collaboration requires a cultural shift within organizations. Leaders must manage this change effectively, addressing employee concerns and fostering a collaborative mindset.

Real-World Examples of Human-Machine Collaboration

Let's explore some real-world examples of human-machine collaboration across different industries:

Healthcare: AI-Assisted Diagnostics

In the healthcare industry, AI is revolutionizing diagnostics. Imagine Dr. Emily, a radiologist at a leading hospital. She works alongside an AI system that analyzes medical images to detect anomalies. The AI system processes thousands of images quickly, highlighting areas of concern for Dr. Emily to review.

This collaboration allows Dr. Emily to focus on interpreting the AI's findings, making more accurate diagnoses, and developing personalized treatment plans. The AI system enhances her capabilities, leading to better patient outcomes.

Finance: Algorithmic Trading

In the finance sector, algorithmic trading is a prime example of human-machine collaboration. Meet Alex, a portfolio manager at an investment firm. Alex uses AI algorithms to analyze market data, identify trends, and execute trades at optimal times.

While the AI handles the data analysis and execution, Alex oversees the overall strategy, adjusting parameters and making decisions based on market conditions. This partnership increases trading efficiency, reduces risks, and maximizes returns.

Manufacturing: Collaborative Robots (Cobots)

In manufacturing, collaborative robots, or cobots, work alongside human workers on assembly lines. Picture Sarah, a worker at a car manufacturing plant. She operates a cobot that assists with assembling car parts.

The cobot handles repetitive tasks like welding and screwing, while Sarah focuses on quality control and complex assembly tasks. This collaboration improves productivity, enhances safety, and allows for more efficient production processes.

Retail: AI-Powered Customer Service

In the retail industry, AI-powered chatbots and virtual assistants enhance customer service. Imagine Chris, a customer service representative at an online retailer. Chris works with an AI chatbot that handles routine inquiries and provides instant responses to customers.

The AI chatbot frees up Chris to address more complex customer issues, build relationships, and provide personalized assistance. This collaboration improves customer satisfaction and reduces response times.

Preparing for Human-Machine Collaboration

To thrive in a world where human-machine collaboration is the norm, individuals and organizations must be proactive in their preparation. Here are some practical steps to get ready:

Invest in Education and Training:

Learn about AI and its applications in your field. Take online courses, attend workshops, and participate in training programs to build your AI literacy.

Organizations should provide ongoing training and development opportunities for employees to ensure they are equipped with the necessary skills to work with AI.

Foster a Collaborative Mindset:

Embrace a mindset that values collaboration and teamwork. Understand that AI is a tool that can enhance your capabilities, not a threat to your job.

Encourage open communication and knowledge sharing within your team. Collaboration thrives in environments where information flows freely and everyone feels valued.

Develop Technical and Soft Skills:

Technical skills are important, but so are soft skills like communication, problem-solving, and adaptability. These skills will enable you to work effectively with AI and contribute to a collaborative environment.

Focus on building a diverse skill set that combines technical proficiency with critical thinking and creativity.

Stay Informed:

Keep up with the latest developments in AI and automation. Follow industry news, read research papers, and join professional networks to stay informed about emerging trends and best practices.

Promote Ethical AI Use:

Advocate for responsible AI use within your organization. Ensure that AI systems are transparent, fair, and aligned with ethical standards.

Establish ethical guidelines and frameworks to address issues such as bias, privacy, and accountability in AI applications.

Hypothetical Future Scenarios

Let's imagine some hypothetical future scenarios to explore the potential of human-machine collaboration:

Scenario 1: AI in Creative Industries

In the future, AI could assist in creative processes such as writing, music composition, and visual arts. Picture a world where an AI collaborator helps writers generate ideas, musicians create melodies, and artists design digital artwork.

Meet Lily, a bestselling author. Lily uses an AI writing assistant to brainstorm plot ideas and develop characters. The AI analyzes vast amounts of literature to suggest unique twists and engaging storylines. Lily's creativity is amplified by the AI's ability to provide fresh perspectives and inspiration.

Scenario 2: AI in Legal Services

AI could revolutionize the legal industry by assisting with research, document analysis, and case preparation. Imagine a scenario where AI systems handle routine legal tasks, allowing lawyers to focus on strategy and client relationships.

Meet David, a corporate lawyer. David's AI assistant reviews contracts, identifies potential issues, and suggests revisions. This collaboration frees up David to provide strategic advice to clients and develop innovative legal solutions. The AI enhances his efficiency and accuracy, making him a more effective lawyer.

Scenario 3: AI in Human Resources

In human resources, AI could streamline recruitment, performance management, and employee engagement. Picture a future where AI systems handle candidate screening, identify top talent, and provide insights into employee satisfaction.

Meet Jessica, an HR manager. Jessica uses an AI-powered recruitment platform to analyze resumes and assess candidates' fit for the company. The AI system also tracks employee performance and suggests personalized development plans. This collaboration allows Jessica to focus on building a positive workplace culture and supporting employees' growth.

Scenario 4: AI in Environmental Conservation

AI could play a crucial role in environmental conservation by monitoring ecosystems, predicting climate patterns, and supporting sustainable practices. Imagine a future where AI systems help scientists and policymakers address environmental challenges.

Meet Dr. Noah, an environmental scientist. Dr. Noah's AI assistant analyzes satellite data to monitor deforestation, predict weather patterns, and identify endangered species' habitats. This collaboration provides valuable insights that inform conservation strategies and policy decisions, helping protect the planet for future generations.

Overcoming Resistance to Human-Machine Collaboration

Embracing human-machine collaboration requires addressing resistance and fostering a culture of acceptance. Here are some strategies to overcome resistance:

Educate and Inform:

Provide education and training to help employees understand the benefits and potential of AI. Clear communication about how AI will enhance their roles can alleviate fears and misconceptions.

Involve Employees in the Process:

Involve employees in the implementation of AI systems. Seek their input, address their concerns, and involve them in decision-making. This collaborative approach can build trust and buy-in.

Highlight Success Stories:

Share success stories and case studies of human-machine collaboration within the organization and industry. Real-world examples can demonstrate the positive impact of AI and inspire confidence.

Provide Support and Resources:

Offer support and resources to help employees transition to new ways of working. This could include training programs, mentorship, and access to AI tools and technologies.

Promote a Positive Narrative:

Promote a positive narrative around AI, emphasizing its potential to enhance human capabilities and create new opportunities. Celebrate achievements and milestones in human-machine collaboration.

Conclusion: Embracing the Future of Teamwork

Human-machine collaboration is transforming the way we work, offering unprecedented opportunities for innovation, productivity, and growth. By understanding the benefits and challenges, preparing proactively, and fostering a collaborative mindset, you can thrive in this new era of teamwork.

Remember, the future of work is not about replacing humans with machines but about creating powerful partnerships that leverage the strengths of both. Embrace this collaboration, stay curious, and be open to learning and adapting. The possibilities are limitless, and with the right approach, you can harness the power of human-machine collaboration to achieve remarkable success.

So, get ready to embark on an exciting journey where humans and machines work together to shape the future. Embrace the potential of this partnership, and you'll be well-prepared to navigate the evolving landscape of work and unlock new opportunities. The future of teamwork is here, and it's brighter than ever.

Chapter 8: Purpose-Driven Work: Finding Meaning in Your Career

The Quest for Meaning

Hello, visionary! By now, you've journeyed through the realms of technology, flexibility, and collaboration. Now, let's dive into a topic that's close to the heart: finding purpose in your work. Imagine waking up every day excited to go to work because you know you're making a difference. That's the power of purpose-driven work.

In this chapter, we'll explore the growing trend of purpose-driven work, why it matters, and how you can find and cultivate purpose in your career. We'll share inspiring stories and practical advice to help you align your work with your values and passions. Ready to embark on this meaningful journey? Let's get started!

Understanding Purpose-Driven Work

Purpose-driven work is about finding meaning and fulfillment in your career. It goes beyond financial rewards and status; it's about contributing to something larger than yourself. Purpose-driven employees feel connected to their work and motivated by a sense of mission and impact.

Key Components of Purpose-Driven Work:

Values Alignment: Your work aligns with your personal values and beliefs.

Passion: You are passionate about what you do and find joy in your work.

Impact: Your work has a positive impact on others, your community, or the world.

Growth: Your work allows for personal and professional growth.

The Importance of Purpose-Driven Work

Purpose-driven work benefits both individuals and organizations. Here's why it's essential:

For Individuals:

Fulfillment: Finding purpose in your work leads to greater job satisfaction and fulfillment. You'll feel more engaged and motivated.

Resilience: Purpose-driven employees are more resilient and better able to navigate challenges and setbacks.

Health and Well-being: Studies show that having a sense of purpose can improve mental and physical health.

For Organizations:

Employee Engagement: Purpose-driven employees are more engaged, productive, and loyal. They're less likely to experience burnout.

Attraction and Retention: Organizations with a clear sense of purpose attract and retain top talent.

Innovation: Purpose-driven companies foster a culture of innovation and creativity, leading to better products and services.

Finding Your Purpose

Finding purpose in your work is a deeply personal journey. Here are some steps to help you discover and cultivate your purpose:

Reflect on Your Values:

Take time to reflect on your core values and beliefs. What matters most to you? What principles guide your decisions and actions?

Consider using tools like the Values in Action (VIA) survey to identify your top values.

Identify Your Passions:

Think about what you love to do. What activities make you feel energized and fulfilled? What topics or causes are you passionate about?

Make a list of your interests and passions. Look for patterns and connections between them.

Explore Your Strengths:

Identify your strengths and skills. What are you naturally good at? What do others often praise you for?

Consider taking strengths assessments like the CliftonStrengths assessment to gain insights into your unique talents.

Define Your Impact:

Consider how you want to make a difference. Who do you want to help? What impact do you want to have on your community or the world?

Write a personal mission statement that captures your purpose and vision for your work.

Experiment and Reflect:

Try new experiences and take on different roles to explore what resonates with you. Volunteer for causes you care about, take on side projects, or seek out new responsibilities at work.

Reflect on your experiences and adjust your path as needed. Purpose is a journey, not a destination.

Cultivating Purpose in Your Current Role

Even if you're not in your dream job, you can find ways to cultivate purpose in your current role. Here are some strategies to help you infuse more meaning into your work:

Align Your Tasks with Your Values:

Look for ways to align your daily tasks with your values. Identify aspects of your job that resonate with your beliefs and focus on those.

Advocate for projects or initiatives that align with your values and passions.

Seek Meaningful Connections:

Build relationships with colleagues who share your values and vision. Collaborate on projects that have a positive impact.

Mentor or support others in their professional growth. Helping others can bring a sense of purpose and fulfillment.

Find Opportunities for Growth:

Seek out opportunities for personal and professional growth. Take on challenging projects, pursue further education, or develop new skills.

Look for ways to innovate and improve processes within your role. Continuous improvement can lead to greater satisfaction and impact.

Contribute to a Larger Mission:

Connect your work to the larger mission of your organization. Understand how your role contributes to the overall goals and impact of the company.

Participate in corporate social responsibility (CSR) initiatives or volunteer programs offered by your organization.

Real-World Examples of Purpose-Driven Work

Let's explore some real-world examples of individuals and organizations that have embraced purpose-driven work:

Patagonia: A Company with a Mission

Patagonia, the outdoor apparel company, is renowned for its commitment to environmental sustainability. Under the leadership of founder Yvon Chouinard, Patagonia's mission is to "build the best product, cause no unnecessary harm, use business to inspire and implement solutions to the environmental crisis."

Employees at Patagonia are driven by a sense of purpose, knowing that their work contributes to protecting the planet. The company's dedication to its mission attracts passionate and committed employees who are aligned with its values.

Dr. Maya: A Purpose-Driven Physician

Dr. Maya, a pediatrician, found her purpose in providing healthcare to underserved communities. After completing her medical training, she joined a nonprofit organization that operates clinics in rural areas.

Dr. Maya's work goes beyond treating illnesses; she educates families on preventive care, advocates for health equity, and mentors young medical professionals. Her sense of purpose fuels her dedication and resilience in the face of challenges.

Ben & Jerry's: Profits and Purpose

Ben & Jerry's, the iconic ice cream company, has built its brand around social justice and environmental sustainability. The company's mission includes a commitment to producing high-quality ice cream while supporting progressive causes.

Employees at Ben & Jerry's are encouraged to engage in activism and community service. The company's purpose-driven approach has created a loyal customer base and a motivated workforce.

Sara: A Social Entrepreneur

Sara, an entrepreneur, founded a company that provides clean drinking water to communities in developing countries. Inspired by her travels and volunteer work, Sara launched a social enterprise that combines business with social impact.

Her company partners with local organizations to install water purification systems and educate communities on hygiene practices. Sara's sense of purpose drives her to expand her impact and innovate solutions for global water challenges.

Hypothetical Future Scenarios

Let's imagine some hypothetical future scenarios to explore the potential of purpose-driven work:

Scenario 1: Tech for Good

In the future, tech companies might increasingly focus on creating products and services that address global challenges. Imagine a tech startup founded by Emma, a software engineer passionate about climate action.

Emma's company develops AI-powered tools that help businesses reduce their carbon footprint. The team is driven by a shared mission to combat climate change, and their innovative solutions gain widespread adoption. Employees find fulfillment in knowing their work contributes to a sustainable future.

Scenario 2: Healthcare Heroes

Picture a future where healthcare professionals prioritize preventive care and community well-being. Dr. David, a physician, leads a clinic focused on holistic health and preventive medicine.

Dr. David's team collaborates with local organizations to offer wellness programs, mental health support, and nutrition education. Patients receive comprehensive care that addresses their physical, mental, and social health. The team's sense of purpose creates a supportive and compassionate environment.

Scenario 3: Corporate Social Responsibility (CSR) Leaders

Imagine a multinational corporation that integrates CSR into its core business strategy. Meet GlobalImpact, a company that manufactures consumer goods with a focus on sustainability and social impact.

CEO Jessica ensures that every aspect of the business, from sourcing materials to production processes, aligns with the company's mission to support sustainable development. Employees are actively involved in CSR initiatives, from volunteering in local communities to participating in environmental conservation projects. The company's purpose-driven culture attracts top talent and loyal customers.

Scenario 4: Education for Empowerment

In the future, education systems might prioritize empowering students to become change-makers. Picture an innovative school founded by Alex, an educator passionate about social justice.

The school's curriculum focuses on critical thinking, empathy, and social entrepreneurship. Students engage in real-world projects that address community issues, from environmental conservation to social equity. Graduates leave with a strong sense of purpose and the skills to make a positive impact in the world.

Practical Steps to Cultivate Purpose

Whether you're seeking to find purpose in your current role or looking to pivot your career, here are some practical steps to help you cultivate purpose:

Engage in Self-Reflection:

Take time to reflect on your values, passions, and strengths. Use journaling, meditation, or conversations with mentors to gain clarity on what drives you.

Set Meaningful Goals:

Define clear and meaningful goals that align with your purpose. Break these goals into actionable steps and track your progress. Celebrate your achievements and learn from setbacks.

Seek Opportunities for Impact:

Look for opportunities to make a positive impact within your role or organization. Volunteer for projects, propose new initiatives, and advocate for causes you care about.

Connect with Like-Minded Individuals:

Build relationships with colleagues, mentors, and community members who share your values and vision. Collaboration and support from like-minded individuals can amplify your impact.

Stay Open to Learning and Growth:

Embrace a growth mindset and continuously seek opportunities for learning and development. Be open to new experiences, challenges, and perspectives that can enrich your journey.

Balance Purpose and Practicality:

While pursuing purpose, consider practical aspects such as financial stability and work-life balance. Strive to find a balance that allows you to sustain your purpose-driven work in the long term.

Conclusion: Embracing Purpose-Driven Work

Purpose-driven work is about more than just a paycheck; it's about making a meaningful impact and finding fulfillment in your career. By aligning your work with your values, passions, and strengths, you can create a career that not only sustains you but also inspires and motivates you.

Remember, the journey to finding and cultivating purpose is ongoing. Stay curious, be open to new opportunities, and continuously reflect on what drives you. Embrace the power of purpose-driven work, and you'll discover a career that brings joy, fulfillment, and a sense of accomplishment.

So, embark on this quest for meaning with enthusiasm and determination. The world needs passionate, purpose-driven individuals like you to make a difference. Embrace your purpose, and let it guide you to a fulfilling and impactful career. The journey ahead is full of possibilities, and with the right approach, you can create a meaningful and inspiring path in the world of work.

Chapter 9: Post-Pandemic Changes: Redefining Normal

A New World Emerges

Hello, resilient reader! As we turn the page to this chapter, we step into a world forever changed by the COVID-19 pandemic. The world was shaken to its core, lives were turned upside down, and the very fabric of our society was altered. In the wake of the pandemic, we are now tasked with redefining what "normal" means.

This chapter will explore the profound changes brought about by the pandemic, the mental health challenges that arose, and provide a roadmap to navigate this new landscape. Through dramatic fictional stories, we'll illuminate the struggles faced by many and offer practical advice to help you overcome these challenges. Ready to redefine your normal? Let's dive in.

The Impact of the Pandemic: A Drastic Shift

The COVID-19 pandemic brought unprecedented disruption to every aspect of life. From the way we work to how we interact with others, nothing was left untouched. Lockdowns, social distancing, and the sudden shift to remote work redefined our daily routines.

Case Study: Emily's Journey Through Isolation

Meet Emily, a marketing executive who thrived in her vibrant office environment. She loved the hustle and bustle of city life, the camaraderie with colleagues, and the structure of her daily routine. When the pandemic hit, Emily found herself confined to her small apartment, cut off from the world she knew.

The days blended into nights, and the once-energizing work became a monotonous grind. Emily struggled with loneliness and anxiety, feeling disconnected from her team and overwhelmed by the constant barrage of bad news. Her mental health began to deteriorate, and she questioned how she could find joy and purpose in this new reality.

Mental Health Challenges: The Invisible Struggle

The pandemic didn't just affect physical health; it also took a severe toll on mental health. Isolation, uncertainty, and the constant fear of illness created a perfect storm for anxiety, depression, and other mental health issues.

Case Study: David's Battle with Anxiety

David, a high school teacher, prided himself on being a source of stability and inspiration for his students. When schools closed, David was forced to transition to online teaching, a medium he was unfamiliar with. The pressure to adapt quickly and effectively was immense.

David began experiencing anxiety attacks, feeling overwhelmed by the sudden changes and the responsibility to support his students remotely. He struggled to sleep, his thoughts raced constantly, and the weight of uncertainty grew heavier each day. David felt like he was losing control and didn't know where to turn for help.

Navigating the New Normal: Strategies for Recovery

While the challenges have been immense, there are ways to navigate this new normal and emerge stronger. Here are some strategies to help you overcome the mental health challenges brought on by the pandemic and redefine your sense of normalcy.

Acknowledge Your Feelings:

It's essential to recognize and validate your emotions. Feeling anxious, sad, or overwhelmed is a natural response to unprecedented changes. Allow yourself to feel and express these emotions without judgment.

Seek Professional Help:

If you're struggling with mental health issues, seek professional support. Therapists, counselors, and mental health professionals can provide guidance and tools to help you cope. Virtual therapy has become more accessible, making it easier to get the support you need.

Build a Support Network:

Stay connected with friends, family, and colleagues. Virtual meetups, phone calls, and online communities can help combat feelings of isolation. Sharing your experiences and hearing from others can provide comfort and perspective.

Establish a Routine:

Creating a daily routine can provide a sense of structure and stability. Set regular work hours, schedule breaks, and include activities that bring you joy and relaxation. A routine helps create a sense of normalcy amidst the chaos.

Practice Self-Care:

Prioritize self-care and well-being. Exercise regularly, eat healthily, and ensure you get enough sleep. Engage in activities that relax and rejuvenate you, whether it's reading, meditating, or pursuing a hobby.

Limit Media Consumption:

Constant exposure to news and social media can heighten anxiety. Set boundaries on media consumption and take breaks from the news. Focus on consuming content that uplifts and inspires you.

Stay Active and Engaged:

Physical activity is a powerful tool for managing stress and improving mood. Find ways to stay active, whether it's through home workouts, outdoor walks, or virtual fitness classes. Staying engaged in meaningful activities can also provide a sense of purpose and fulfillment.

Adapting to New Work Models

The pandemic has permanently altered the way we work. As we move forward, hybrid work models and increased flexibility will become the norm. Here's how you can adapt and thrive in this new work environment.

Embrace Flexibility:

Be open to flexible work arrangements, whether it's remote work, hybrid models, or flexible hours. Embracing flexibility allows you to find a work-life balance that suits your needs.

Leverage Technology:

Utilize digital tools and platforms to enhance productivity and collaboration. Familiarize yourself with video conferencing, project management software, and communication tools to stay connected with your team.

Create a Productive Workspace:

Set up a dedicated workspace that minimizes distractions and enhances focus. Ensure you have the necessary equipment and a comfortable environment to work efficiently.

Prioritize Communication:

Effective communication is crucial in remote and hybrid work models. Maintain regular check-ins with your team, provide updates, and seek feedback. Clear and consistent communication fosters collaboration and understanding.

Set Boundaries:

Establish boundaries between work and personal life to prevent burnout. Define your work hours, take breaks, and unplug after work. Setting boundaries helps maintain a healthy work-life balance.

Continue Learning and Development:

Invest in continuous learning and development. Take advantage of online courses, webinars, and training programs to enhance your skills and stay competitive in the evolving job market.

Finding New Sources of Joy and Fulfillment

As we redefine normal, it's essential to find new sources of joy and fulfillment. Here are some ways to discover happiness and purpose in this new landscape.

Explore New Hobbies:

Take up new hobbies or rekindle old ones. Whether it's painting, cooking, gardening, or playing a musical instrument, engaging in activities you enjoy can bring joy and satisfaction.

Volunteer and Give Back:

Volunteering and helping others can provide a sense of purpose and fulfillment. Look for opportunities to support your community, whether it's through virtual volunteering or local initiatives.

Practice Mindfulness and Gratitude:

Mindfulness practices like meditation and deep breathing can help you stay grounded and present. Practicing gratitude by acknowledging the positives in your life can improve your mental well-being.

Connect with Nature:

Spending time in nature can have a calming and rejuvenating effect. Whether it's a walk in the park, a hike, or simply sitting in your garden, nature can provide a much-needed escape from daily stresses.

Pursue Personal Goals:

Set personal goals that align with your passions and values. Whether it's learning a new skill, writing a book, or starting a side project, pursuing personal goals can bring a sense of accomplishment and purpose.

Case Study: Anna's Path to Rediscovery

Meet Anna, a graphic designer who thrived in her creative agency. The pandemic forced her to work from home, and she struggled with the lack of social interaction and creative inspiration. Anna's mental health began to decline, and she felt disconnected from her work and colleagues.

Determined to find a new sense of purpose, Anna decided to explore her passion for photography. She started a daily photo journal, capturing moments of beauty in her surroundings. This new hobby reignited her creativity and provided a sense of fulfillment.

Anna also began volunteering for a local animal shelter, using her design skills to create promotional materials. The combination of photography and volunteering brought joy and purpose back into her life. She found that by embracing new interests and giving back to her community, she could overcome the challenges brought by the pandemic and rediscover her passion.

Conclusion: Redefining Normal

The COVID-19 pandemic has changed our world in profound ways. As we navigate this new landscape, it's essential to redefine what normal means for us individually and collectively. By acknowledging the mental health challenges, adapting to new work models, and finding new sources of joy and fulfillment, we can emerge stronger and more resilient.

Remember, redefining normal is a personal journey. Stay connected with your values, seek support when needed, and embrace new opportunities for growth and discovery. The journey ahead is filled with uncertainty, but also with potential for renewal and transformation.

So, take a deep breath, embrace the change, and chart your path forward. The world may have changed, but your ability to find meaning and purpose remains. Redefine your normal, and you'll create a life that is fulfilling, joyful, and resilient. The future is yours to shape.

Chapter 10: Conclusion: Preparing for the Future

Navigating Economic Instability

Welcome, steadfast reader, to the final chapter of our journey. As we stand on the precipice of the future, it's impossible to ignore the economic instability that looms large over America, Canada, and many other parts of the world. The landscape is marked by recession fears, layoffs, and the falling economies of numerous countries. But amid this uncertainty, there lies a horizon of hope and opportunity for those who are prepared and skill-ready.

In this chapter, we will explore the current economic challenges and then turn our gaze toward a brighter future. We will provide insights on how to navigate these turbulent times and offer a motivational outlook for what lies ahead. Together, let's chart a course through the storm and toward the sunrise of new possibilities.

Economic Instability: The Current Landscape

The global economy has been under significant strain, exacerbated by the COVID-19 pandemic, geopolitical tensions, and various internal challenges. Let's delve into the specific issues facing the economies of America, Canada, and beyond.

Recession and Economic Slowdown:

Both the United States and Canada have experienced economic slowdowns, with periods of negative growth. The pandemic disrupted supply chains, decreased consumer spending, and led to widespread business closures.

The ripple effects of these disruptions are still being felt, with many industries struggling to recover. Key sectors such as hospitality, travel, and retail have been particularly hard hit.

Layoffs and Unemployment:

Layoffs have become a harsh reality for many workers. Companies across various sectors have had to downsize to survive, leading to increased unemployment rates.

The gig economy, while providing some relief, is not immune to these challenges. Gig workers often face instability and lack of benefits, making economic resilience difficult.

Global Economic Challenges:

The economic woes are not confined to North America. Many countries around the world are grappling with similar issues, from recession to inflation.

Emerging markets have been particularly vulnerable, with economic crises leading to social unrest and further instability.

Case Study: Alex's Struggle with Job Loss

Meet Alex, a software engineer at a mid-sized tech firm in Toronto. For years, Alex enjoyed a stable career, working on exciting projects and climbing the corporate ladder. Then the pandemic hit, and his company faced severe financial difficulties. Despite their best efforts, the firm had to lay off a significant portion of its workforce, and Alex found himself among those affected.

The sudden job loss was a blow to Alex's confidence and financial stability. He struggled with feelings of uncertainty and fear for the future. The job market was saturated with similarly qualified professionals, and finding new employment seemed daunting. Alex's story is a reflection of the harsh realities faced by many during these tumultuous times.

The Dawn of a New Era: Skills for the Future

Despite the economic instability, there is hope. The future holds immense potential for those who are prepared, adaptable, and ready to embrace new opportunities. Here's how you can equip yourself to thrive in the changing landscape.

Embrace Lifelong Learning:

The ability to continuously learn and adapt is crucial. Take advantage of online courses, workshops, and certifications to stay current with industry trends and acquire new skills.

Focus on both hard skills (such as data analysis, coding, and digital marketing) and soft skills (such as communication, critical thinking, and emotional intelligence).

Diversify Your Skill Set:

Having a diverse skill set increases your employability and resilience. Consider learning complementary skills that enhance your primary expertise.

For example, if you're in marketing, learning about data analytics or graphic design can make you more versatile and valuable.

Network and Build Relationships:

Networking is more important than ever. Build and maintain professional relationships through virtual events, social media, and industry forums.

Join professional organizations, attend webinars, and engage with thought leaders in your field to expand your network and uncover new opportunities.

Embrace Technology:

Technology is a driving force in the modern economy. Familiarize yourself with emerging technologies and how they can be applied in your field.

Whether it's AI, blockchain, or cybersecurity, understanding technological advancements will give you a competitive edge.

Adapt to Remote and Hybrid Work:

The shift to remote and hybrid work models is likely to persist. Develop the skills needed to thrive in these environments, such as effective communication, time management, and self-discipline.

Invest in a reliable home office setup and familiarize yourself with collaboration tools to stay productive and connected.

Focus on Resilience and Well-Being:

Personal resilience and well-being are crucial for navigating uncertain times. Practice self-care, maintain a healthy work-life balance, and seek support when needed.

Build mental and emotional resilience by engaging in activities that reduce stress and promote well-being, such as exercise, mindfulness, and hobbies.

Case Study: Mia's Journey to Resilience

Meet Mia, a marketing professional in New York City. When the pandemic hit, Mia's company faced severe financial difficulties, and she was laid off. Initially devastated, Mia decided to view the setback as an opportunity to reinvent herself.

Mia enrolled in online courses to learn about digital marketing and data analytics. She attended virtual networking events and connected with industry professionals. Through perseverance and adaptability, Mia landed a remote job with a tech startup that values her new skill set. Her journey from despair to resilience is a testament to the power of adaptability and continuous learning.

A Motivational Sunrise: The Future Awaits

Despite the challenges, the future holds promise for those who are prepared and adaptable. Economic instability may create turbulence, but it also opens the door to innovation, growth, and new opportunities. Here's why you should feel hopeful about the future:

Innovation and Entrepreneurship:

Economic challenges often spur innovation. As businesses adapt to new realities, opportunities for entrepreneurship and innovation arise.

New startups and business models will emerge, creating jobs and driving economic growth. By staying attuned to market needs and trends, you can position yourself to capitalize on these opportunities.

Global Connectivity:

The world is more connected than ever before. Global collaboration and remote work have opened up new possibilities for cross-border partnerships and international careers.

Embrace the global workforce and explore opportunities beyond your local market. Your next career move might be in a different country or continent.

Focus on Sustainability:

The push for sustainability and environmental responsibility is gaining momentum. Companies are increasingly focusing on green technologies and sustainable practices.

Skills related to sustainability, renewable energy, and environmental management will be in high demand. Align your career with these growing fields to make a positive impact and secure your future.

The Rise of the Gig Economy:

The gig economy offers flexibility and diverse opportunities. Freelancing, consulting, and project-based work allow you to diversify your income streams and gain experience across different industries.

Embrace the gig economy as a way to build resilience and explore various career paths. Platforms like Upwork, Fiverr, and Freelancer offer access to a global marketplace of opportunities.

Empowerment Through Technology:

Technology empowers individuals to create, innovate, and connect. Leverage digital tools to build your personal brand, showcase your skills, and reach new audiences.

Whether you're a freelancer, entrepreneur, or remote worker, technology provides the resources you need to succeed and thrive in the modern economy.

Conclusion: Embracing the Future

As we conclude this journey, remember that the future is not something to fear but to embrace. The economic landscape may be uncertain, but with the right skills, mindset, and resilience, you can navigate these challenges and seize new opportunities.

Stay committed to lifelong learning, diversify your skill set, and build a strong professional network. Embrace technology, adapt to new work models, and focus on personal well-being. By doing so, you'll be well-prepared to thrive in the evolving world of work.

So, as you look toward the horizon, envision a future filled with possibilities and promise. The sun may set on old ways, but it rises on new beginnings. Embrace the sunrise, and let it guide you to a fulfilling and prosperous future. The journey ahead is yours to shape, and with the right approach, you can achieve remarkable success.

Thank you for joining me on this journey. Here's to a bright and hopeful future, ready for skill-ready folks like you. The best is yet to come.

Chapter 11: Preparing for an Unpredictable World: Strategies for Resilience and Adaptability

Embracing the Unknown

Hello, seeker of wisdom! As we stand at the threshold of an unpredictable world, it's natural to feel a mix of apprehension and excitement. Life is a journey filled with twists and turns, and the path ahead may be uncertain. But it is in this very uncertainty that the seeds of resilience and adaptability are sown. This chapter will guide you through the philosophical underpinnings of navigating an unpredictable world, offering motivational insights and practical strategies to thrive.

In this concluding chapter, we will reflect on the lessons learned, revisit key concepts, and explore profound strategies to build resilience and adaptability. Together, we will uncover the wisdom needed to face the unknown with courage and grace. Ready to embark on this final journey? Let's dive in.

The Philosophical Journey: Embracing Change and Uncertainty

Life is an ever-changing tapestry, woven with threads of unpredictability and transformation. Embracing this change is not merely a necessity but a profound aspect of the human experience. Throughout history, great thinkers and philosophers have pondered the nature of change and the importance of resilience. Let's explore some of their timeless wisdom.

The Wisdom of Heraclitus:

The ancient Greek philosopher Heraclitus famously said, "The only constant in life is change." This simple yet profound truth reminds us that change is inevitable and ever-present. Embracing this reality allows us to flow with the currents of life rather than resist them.

The Stoic Perspective:

Stoicism, a school of philosophy founded in ancient Greece, teaches the importance of accepting what we cannot control and focusing on what we can. The Stoics believed that inner peace comes from aligning our will with the natural order of the universe. As Marcus Aurelius wrote, "The universe is change; our life is what our thoughts make it."

Buddhist Teachings:

Buddhism emphasizes the impermanence of all things. The understanding that everything is transient and subject to change helps us cultivate a mindset of detachment and acceptance. As the Buddha taught, "Everything changes, nothing remains without change."

The Power of Resilience: Bouncing Back Stronger

Resilience is the ability to bounce back from adversity, to recover and thrive despite challenges. It is a vital trait that enables us to navigate the unpredictability of life with strength and grace. Here are some philosophical insights and practical strategies to build resilience.

Cultivating Inner Strength:

Resilience begins within. Cultivate inner strength by nurturing your mental and emotional well-being. Practices such as meditation, mindfulness, and journaling can help you develop a strong and centered mind.

Finding Meaning in Adversity:

Adversity can be a powerful teacher. Find meaning in difficult experiences by reflecting on the lessons they offer. Viktor Frankl, a Holocaust survivor and psychiatrist, wrote about the importance of finding meaning in suffering in his book "Man's Search for Meaning." He believed that meaning is the key to resilience.

Building a Support Network:

Resilience is not built in isolation. Surround yourself with supportive and uplifting individuals who encourage and inspire you. Build a network of friends, family, mentors, and colleagues who can provide guidance and support during challenging times.

Developing a Growth Mindset:

A growth mindset, as described by psychologist Carol Dweck, is the belief that abilities and intelligence can be developed through effort and learning. Embrace challenges as opportunities for growth and view failures as stepping stones to success.

Case Study: The Resilient Journey of Leah

Meet Leah, a single mother and entrepreneur. Leah's journey has been fraught with challenges, from financial struggles to personal setbacks. Yet, through it all, she has demonstrated remarkable resilience.

Leah's business faced a major downturn during the economic recession. With bills piling up and her future uncertain, Leah felt overwhelmed. But instead of succumbing to despair, she decided to draw upon her inner strength and resilience.

Leah began practicing mindfulness and journaling daily, finding clarity and peace amidst the chaos. She reached out to her network for support and guidance, receiving invaluable advice from mentors and friends. With a growth mindset, Leah adapted her business model, exploring new markets and innovative solutions.

Through perseverance and adaptability, Leah's business began to recover and thrive. Her journey is a testament to the power of resilience and the importance of finding meaning and support in times of adversity.

The Art of Adaptability: Thriving in an Ever-Changing World

Adaptability is the ability to adjust to new conditions and environments. In an unpredictable world, adaptability is essential for survival and success. Let's explore philosophical insights and practical strategies to cultivate adaptability.

Embracing Flexibility:

Adaptability requires flexibility in thought and action. Be open to new ideas, perspectives, and approaches. As the saying goes, "Blessed are the flexible, for they shall not be bent out of shape."

Living in the Present Moment:

The ability to adapt is rooted in being present. Focus on the here and now, and respond to current circumstances rather than worrying about the past or future. Mindfulness practices can help you stay grounded and adaptable.

Learning from Nature:

Nature is the ultimate teacher of adaptability. Observe how plants and animals adapt to their environments, finding ways to thrive despite challenges. As Charles Darwin noted, "It is not the strongest of the species that survive, nor the most intelligent, but the one most responsive to change."

Continuous Learning and Growth:

Adaptability is fueled by a commitment to continuous learning. Stay curious and seek out new knowledge and experiences. Embrace lifelong learning as a way to stay adaptable and responsive to change.

Case Study: Ethan's Path to Adaptability

Meet Ethan, a software developer who thrived in the fast-paced tech industry. When the company he worked for underwent a major restructuring, Ethan found himself at a crossroads. His role was being phased out, and he needed to adapt quickly to the changing landscape.

Ethan decided to embrace the uncertainty as an opportunity for growth. He enrolled in online courses to learn new programming languages and technologies. He also began networking with industry professionals to explore new career paths.

As Ethan immersed himself in continuous learning, he discovered a passion for artificial intelligence and machine learning. He pivoted his career and joined a startup focused on AI development. Ethan's adaptability and willingness to embrace change led to a fulfilling and successful new chapter in his career.

Building Resilience and Adaptability: Practical Strategies

Now that we've explored the philosophical foundations of resilience and adaptability, let's dive into practical strategies to cultivate these traits in your life.

Practice Mindfulness and Meditation:

Mindfulness and meditation can help you stay grounded and present, enhancing your ability to adapt to changing circumstances. Set aside time each day to practice mindfulness, focusing on your breath and observing your thoughts without judgment.

Set Realistic Goals:

Set realistic and achievable goals that align with your values and aspirations. Break larger goals into smaller, manageable steps, and celebrate your progress along the way. Setting goals gives you a sense of direction and purpose.

Develop Emotional Intelligence:

Emotional intelligence is the ability to understand and manage your emotions and the emotions of others. Cultivate emotional intelligence by practicing self-awareness, empathy, and effective communication. These skills will enhance your resilience and adaptability.

Embrace Change as an Opportunity:

View change as an opportunity for growth and learning rather than a threat. Embrace new experiences, challenges, and perspectives with an open mind. Adopting a positive attitude towards change will help you navigate it more effectively.

Build a Support System:

Surround yourself with supportive individuals who uplift and inspire you. Build a network of friends, family, mentors, and colleagues who can provide guidance, encouragement, and support during challenging times.

Stay Physically Active:

Physical activity is a powerful tool for managing stress and building resilience. Incorporate regular exercise into your routine, whether it's through walking, running, yoga, or other forms of physical activity. Staying active will improve your overall well-being.

Practice Gratitude:

Cultivate an attitude of gratitude by regularly reflecting on the positive aspects of your life. Keep a gratitude journal, noting the things you are thankful for each day. Practicing gratitude can enhance your resilience and overall outlook on life.

Case Study: The Transformative Journey of Maria

Meet Maria, a nurse working in a busy urban hospital. The COVID-19 pandemic brought unprecedented challenges to her profession, testing her resilience and adaptability. Maria witnessed the suffering of patients, the exhaustion of her colleagues, and the overwhelming demands of her job.

Despite the hardships, Maria found strength in her sense of purpose and commitment to her patients. She practiced mindfulness and meditation to stay grounded and focused. Maria also sought support from her colleagues, sharing experiences and offering encouragement.

To enhance her adaptability, Maria enrolled in courses on healthcare management and leadership. She embraced continuous learning and sought innovative ways to improve patient care. Maria's resilience and adaptability not only helped her navigate the challenges of the pandemic but also led to her promotion to a leadership role.

Maria's journey is a powerful reminder that resilience and adaptability are cultivated through practice, support, and a commitment to personal growth.

Reflecting on the Journey: Key Takeaways

As we conclude this chapter and our journey together, let's reflect on the key takeaways that will guide you in preparing for an unpredictable world.

Embrace Change:

Change is a constant in life. Embrace it with an open mind and a positive attitude. View change as an opportunity for growth and transformation.

Cultivate Resilience:

Resilience is the ability to bounce back from adversity. Cultivate resilience by building inner strength, finding meaning in challenges, and seeking support from others.

Develop Adaptability:

Adaptability is the ability to adjust to new conditions. Develop adaptability by embracing flexibility, staying present, and committing to continuous learning.

Practice Mindfulness:

Mindfulness helps you stay grounded and present, enhancing your resilience and adaptability. Practice mindfulness and meditation regularly to cultivate a centered mind.

Build a Support Network:

Surround yourself with supportive and uplifting individuals. Build a network of friends, family, mentors, and colleagues who can provide guidance and encouragement.

Focus on Well-Being:

Prioritize your mental, emotional, and physical well-being. Engage in activities that reduce stress, promote health, and bring joy.

Stay Curious and Open:

Stay curious and open to new experiences, ideas, and perspectives. Embrace lifelong learning as a way to stay adaptable and responsive to change.

A Motivational Sunrise: The Future is Bright

As we stand on the brink of an unpredictable world, remember that the future is bright for those who are prepared and adaptable. The journey may be filled with challenges, but it is also rich with opportunities for growth, innovation, and fulfillment.

Envision a future where you navigate the currents of change with grace and resilience, where you embrace new experiences with curiosity and openness, and where you find meaning and purpose in every step of your journey. The path ahead is yours to shape, and with the right approach, you can achieve remarkable success.

Final Reflections

Thank you for joining me on this transformative journey. Together, we've explored the future of work, the rise of remote work and the gig economy, the impact of AI, the pursuit of purpose-driven work, and the importance of resilience and adaptability. Each chapter has offered insights and strategies to help you thrive in an ever-changing world.

As you move forward, carry these lessons with you. Embrace the unknown, cultivate resilience and adaptability, and stay committed to personal growth and well-being. The future is filled with endless possibilities, and with the wisdom you've gained, you are well-equipped to navigate it with confidence and grace.

Here's to a bright and hopeful future, ready for skill-ready folks like you. The best is yet to come.

Epilogue

As we conclude our journey through "Work 2.0: Preparing For the Future Jobs," I hope you feel inspired and equipped to navigate the dynamic landscape of the future work environment. The world is changing rapidly, and with these changes come both challenges and opportunities. Embracing the future of work means being proactive, adaptable, and committed to lifelong learning.

In this book, we've delved into the remote work revolution, the essential skills needed for jobs that don't yet exist, the gig economy, the impact of automation and AI, the rise of digital nomadism, organizational adaptation, human-machine collaboration, purpose-driven work, and the post-pandemic changes redefining normal. Each chapter has provided insights, practical advice, and real-world examples to help you prepare for the evolving job market.

As you move forward, remember that the key to success in this new era is a combination of technical proficiency and human-centric skills. Digital literacy, emotional intelligence, critical thinking, adaptability, and a growth mindset will be your most valuable assets. These skills will not only help you stay relevant but also enable you to thrive in an ever-changing world.

Embrace Change with Confidence

Change can be daunting, but it also brings endless possibilities. Embrace it with confidence and view every challenge as an opportunity for growth. Stay curious and open to new experiences. Seek out learning opportunities, whether through online courses, workshops, or hands-on experiences. The more you learn, the better prepared you'll be to tackle the future.

Cultivate a Sense of Purpose

Finding meaning in your work can be a powerful motivator. Reflect on your values, passions, and strengths to identify what truly matters to you. Align your career goals with your personal mission, and seek out roles that allow you to make a positive impact. Purpose-driven work can lead to greater job satisfaction, resilience, and overall well-being.

Build a Supportive Network

Surround yourself with like-minded individuals who share your vision and values. Build a supportive network of mentors, colleagues, and friends who can offer guidance, encouragement, and collaboration. Together, you can navigate the complexities of the future work environment and achieve remarkable success.

Stay Agile and Resilient

The future is unpredictable, and the ability to adapt to changing circumstances is crucial. Stay agile and resilient by developing a diverse skill set, maintaining a healthy work-life balance, and prioritizing your well-being. Embrace new technologies and be open to pivoting your career as needed.

A Call to Action

The future of work is bright and full of potential. As you embark on this journey, take proactive steps to prepare yourself for the jobs of tomorrow. Invest in your education, cultivate your skills, and remain adaptable in the face of change. The possibilities are limitless, and with the right mindset and preparation, you can shape a fulfilling and successful career.

Thank you for joining me on this exploration of the future of work. I wish you all the best as you navigate the exciting opportunities ahead. Embrace the future with confidence, curiosity, and a commitment to lifelong learning. The world is waiting for your unique contributions, and I have no doubt that you will make a significant impact.

Bushra Siddiqui

Felix McKenzie

www.ingramcontent.com/pod-product-compliance
Lightning Source LLC
Chambersburg PA
CBHW050109230526
45470CB00004B/1741